HEATH
ALGEBRA 1
AN INTEGRATED APPROACH
LARSON, KANOLD, STIFF

EXTRA PRACTICE
COPYMASTERS

Cheryl Leech

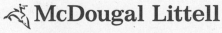

McDougal Littell

Evanston, Illinois • Boston • Dallas

D0813871

International Standard Book Number: 0-395-87196-4

2 3 4 5 6 7 8 9 10 HWI 01 00 99 98

1.1

Name _____

In 1–12, use mental math.

1. What is the sum of 3 and 6?

2. What is the sum of 14 and 4?

3. What is the sum of 5 and 8?

4. What is the difference of 7 and 3?

5. What is the difference of 12 and 6?

6. What is the difference of 10 and 1?

7. What is the product of 2 and 9?

8. What is the product of 6 and 4?

9. What is the product of 4 and 4?

10. What is the quotient of 27 and 9?

11. What is the quotient of 15 and 3?

12. What is the quotient of 35 and 5?

In 13–24, evaluate the expression.

13. $[10 - (4 \cdot 2)] \cdot 3$

14. $4 + [(3 \cdot 4) - 5]$

15. $14 - [(2 \cdot 6) + 1]$

16. $[(4 \cdot 4) + 2] + 4$

17. $8 + [49 \div (3 + 4)]$

18. $11 - [48 \div (4 \cdot 2)]$

19. $[12 - (12 \div 2)] + 3$

20. $[18 \div (2 + 1)] - 4$

21. $24 \div [(4 \cdot 3) - 6]$

22. $[100 \div (5 \cdot 2)] + 3$

23. $[(3 \cdot 3) + 12] \div 7$

24. $36 \div [12 - (6 \div 2)]$

Geometry **In 25–27, find the perimeter of the figure.**

25.
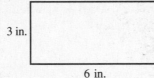
3 in.

6 in.

26.
2 in.

8 in.

27.
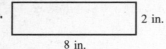
1 in.

5 in.

28. ***Campaign Posters*** You are running for Student Council president and you want to make campaign posters. Each poster will have a height of 2 ft and a width of 1 ft. If you make 8 posters, how many square feet of poster paper do you need?

2 ft

1 ft

29. ***Sandbox Construction*** You are making a sandbox for your younger brother. The width of the sandbox is 3 ft and its length is 4 ft. How much will it cost to construct the boundary of the sandbox if the wood you are using costs $2 per foot?

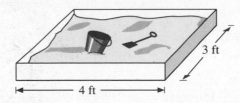
3 ft

4 ft

30. ***Library Fines*** You borrowed three books from the library. All three books were due two days ago. If the fine for late return is 5¢ per day, how much money do you owe if you return the books today?

Total Owed	=	Number of Books	·	Fine per Book per Day	·	Number of Days

1.2

Name _____

In 1–24, evaluate the expression.

1. $x + 5$, when $x = 4$

2. $y - 4$, when $y = 19$

3. $3x + 2$, when $x = 2$

4. $5w + 8$, when $w = 3$

5. $7 - 2x$, when $x = 2$

6. $3a + 4b$, when $a = 3$ and $b = 1$

7. $6c - d$, when $c = 2$ and $d = 10$

8. $4w - s + 2$, when $w = 2$ and $s = 7$

9. $11 + 3x - 5y$, when $x = 1$ and $y = 2$

10. $(a + 3) + 2b$, when $a = 1$ and $b = 2$

11. $9a - (2 + b)$, when $a = 1$ and $b = 6$

12. $3x + (x - 4)$, when $x = 6$

13. $(2y + 6) - 4y$, when $y = 3$

14. $5c - (2 + c)$, when $c = 2$

15. $2b(7 + b)$, when $b = 1$

16. $(3x + 1)x$, when $x = 3$

17. $3x(2y - 3)$, when $x = 5$ and $y = 2$

18. $3x + 2(2x + 5)$, when $x = 1$

19. $15 \div (2a + 1)$, when $a = 1$

20. $(7x + 4) \div 2$, when $x = 2$

21. $x \div (2y + 1)$, when $x = 21$ and $y = 1$

22. $b \div (3a - 2)$, when $a = 2$ and $b = 16$

23. $(6a + 2) \div b$, when $a = 3$ and $b = 2$

24. $[10 - (2x \div 3)] + y$, when $x = 3$ and $y = 4$

25. *Geometry* A trapezoid is a 4-sided polygon which has 2 parallel sides.
a. Write an expression that represents the perimeter of a trapezoid whose sides have lengths a, b, c, and d. Use this expression to find the perimeter of each trapezoid.

b.
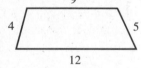

c.
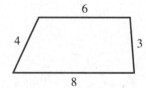

d.
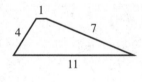

26. *Interest* Suppose you deposit $100.00 in a savings account that pays an annual rate of 5%. How much interest would you earn in 6 months?

| Interest | = | Amount of Deposit | · | Interest Rate (decimal) | · | Time (years) |

27. *Temperature Conversion* You are performing a chemistry experiment. You know that water freezes at $0°$C, but your thermometer measures temperature in degrees Fahrenheit. At what temperature in degrees Fahrenheit will water freeze?

| Temperature ($°$F) | = | $\frac{9}{5}$ | · | Temperature ($°$C) | + | 32 |

In 1–12, write the expression in exponential form.

1. Three to the fourth power   **2.** Seven squared   **3.** x cubed

4. y to the fifth power   **5.** 3 to the w power   **6.** $6x$ cubed

7. $4 \cdot 4 \cdot 4 \cdot 4 \cdot 4$ **8.** $a \cdot a \cdot a$ **9.** $2 \cdot 2$

10. $x \cdot x \cdot x \cdot x \cdot x \cdot x \cdot x \cdot x$ **11.** $5 \cdot 5 \cdot 5 \cdot 5$ **12.** $3x \cdot 3x \cdot 3x \cdot 3x$

In 13–24, evaluate the expression.

13. x^3, when $x = 2$ **14.** a^2, when $a = 10$ **15.** $y^3 - 5$, when $y = 2$

16. $6 + x^2$, when $x = 5$ **17.** $14 - y^2$, when $y = 3$ **18.** $(x - y)^4$, when $x = 5$ and $y = 3$

19. $a^2 + b^3$, when $a = 7$ and $b = 1$ **20.** $a + b^3$, when $a = 3$ and $b = 2$ **21.** $(7x - 8)^2$, when $x = 2$

22. $(3x - 6)^3$, when $x = 3$ **23.** $4a^2 + 2b$, when $a = 2$ and $b = 3$ **24.** $(2y)^2 - x^2$, when $x = 3$ and $y = 2$

25. *Beach Ball* When blown up, a beach ball has a radius of 1 ft. How much air is needed to blow up the beach ball? (The volume of a sphere is $V = \frac{4}{3}\pi r^3$ where $\pi \approx 3.14$ and r is the radius.)

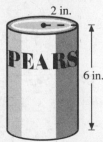

26. *Safe Storage* A safe has a cubical storage space inside. What is the volume of a safe with an interior length of 2 ft?

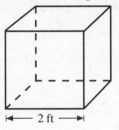

27. *Cylindrical Can* An aluminum can has a radius of 2 in. and a height of 6 in. What is the volume of the can? (The volume of a cylinder is $V = \pi r^2 h$ where $\pi \approx 3.14$, r is the radius, and h is the height.)

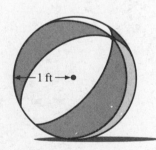

28. *Area Rug* A circular area rug has a radius of 3 ft. How much area does the rug cover? (The area of a circle is $A = \pi r^2$ where $\pi \approx 3.14$ and r is the radius.)

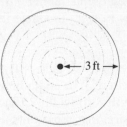

In 1–12, evaluate the expression.

1. $5 + 2 - 3$

2. $12 - 6 + 1$

3. $10 \cdot 2 \div 4$

4. $4 + 3 \cdot 2$

5. $8 \cdot 3 - 10$

6. $5 - 14 \div 7$

7. $2 + 36 \div 4$

8. $10 \div 5 + 3 \cdot 2$

9. $4 - 20 \div 10 + 7$

10. $3 \cdot 2^2 + 1$

11. $2 \cdot 3^2 \div 3$

12. $4(2 + 3) - 18$

In 13–24, evaluate the expression.

13. $3 + 2x^2$, when $x = 2$

14. $30 - 3x^2$, when $x = 3$

15. $3a - 2b$, when $a = 2$ and $b = 3$

16. $5x^2 - y$, when $x = 3$ and $y = 5$

17. $2x + x^2 - 4$, when $x = 4$

18. $a^3 - 3a + 5$, when $a = 2$

19. $a^2 \div 5 + 3$, when $a = 5$

20. $x \cdot y - 8$, when $x = 3$ and $y = 4$

21. $a^2 - b \div 4$, when $a = 5$ and $b = 8$

22. $3y - x^2 \cdot 4$, when $x = 2$ and $y = 6$

23. $\dfrac{2a + b}{3}$, when $a = 4$ and $b = 1$

24. $7 - \dfrac{x}{y} \cdot 2$, when $x = 15$ and $y = 5$

Technology In 25–28, two calculators were used to evaluate the expression. They gave different results. Which calculator used the established order of operations?

25. $12 \boxed{-} 4 \boxed{\times} 2 \boxed{+} 1 \boxed{=}$

Calculator 1: 5   Calculator 2: 17

26. $5 \boxed{\times} 3 \boxed{-} 4 \boxed{\times} 2 \boxed{=}$

Calculator 1: 7   Calculator 2: 22

27. $2 \boxed{\times} 6 \boxed{+} 3 \boxed{\div} 3 \boxed{=}$

Calculator 1: 5   Calculator 2: 13

28. $10 \boxed{-} 5 \boxed{\times} 4 \boxed{\div} 10 \boxed{=}$

Calculator: 1: 8   Calculator 2: 2

29. *Shotput* During a track meet, Kelly throws the shotput 51 ft, 50 ft, and 58 ft. Write an expression that represents the length of his average throw in feet. Evaluate the expression.

30. *Sales Tax* You want to buy a newly released CD. The CD costs $17 plus 6% tax. Write an expression that represents how much money in dollars you need to buy the CD. Evaluate the expression.

31. *Fish Tank* You have two fish tanks. The first has a length of 4 ft, a width of 2 ft, and a height of 3 ft. The second has length 3 ft, width 2 ft, and height 1 ft. Write an expression that represents the amount of water in cubic feet both tanks will hold. Evaluate the expression.

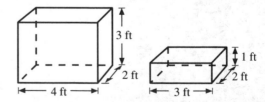

Algebra 1

In 1–9, check whether the given number is a solution of the equation.

1. $2x + 3 = 7, \ 4$

2. $4x + 2 = 10, \ 1$

3. $3x - 5 = 1, \ 2$

4. $6 = 2x - 8, \ 6$

5. $17 - 4a = 13, \ 1$

6. $5a - 3 = 2a, \ 3$

7. $4y - 6 = 2y, \ 3$

8. $y + 3y = 2y + 4, \ 3$

9. $5x + 3 = x + 7, \ 1$

In 10–18, write a question that could be used to solve the equation. Then use mental math to solve the equation.

10. $x - 5 = 3$

11. $x + 2 = 6$

12. $x + 4 = 6$

13. $x - 2 = 5$

14. $4x = 20$

15. $3x = 9$

16. $\dfrac{x}{2} = 3$

17. $\dfrac{x}{3} = 4$

18. $x^3 = 8$

In 19–27, check whether the given number is a solution of the inequality.

19. $x - 5 \leq 7, \ 9$

20. $x + 3 > 8, \ 4$

21. $3 + x < 8, \ 5$

22. $10 - x > 2, \ 9$

23. $2x + 1 \geq 10, \ 6$

24. $4x - 3 \leq 5, \ 2$

25. $2x - 3 < 0, \ 2$

26. $6x + 1 \geq 8x - 7, \ 2$

27. $5x + 1 \geq x - 3, \ 4$

Locker Installation Suppose your school is replacing some of its lockers. When the old lockers are removed there is a space 144 in. long. Each new locker has a width of 8 in. How many new lockers can be installed?

28. If this problem is represented by the equation $8x = 144$, what do the 8, x, and 144 represent?

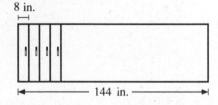

8 in.

|← 144 in. →|

Statue of Liberty The Statue of Liberty's torch has 14 lamps that give off 14,000 watts of light. If all the lamps are identical, how many watts are given off in one lamp?

29. If this problem is represented by the equation $14x = 14,000$, what do the 14, x, and 14,000 represent?

Layers of Earth Earth's radius is approximately 4,010 miles. The crust is approximately 10 miles wide, the mantle is approximately 1800 miles wide, and the inner core has a radius of approximately 800 miles. What is the width of the outer core?

30. If this problem is represented by the equation $10 + 1800 + x + 800 = 4010$, what do the 10, 1800, x, 800, and 4010 represent?

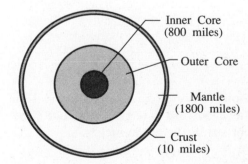

Inner Core (800 miles)

Outer Core

Mantle (1800 miles)

Crust (10 miles)

In 1–12, translate the phrase into an algebraic expression.

1. 4 more than a number

2. 6 less than a number

3. The difference of 7 and a number

4. The sum of a number and 2

5. 5 times a given number

6. One third of a given number

7. A number divided by 8

8. 9 more than twice a given number

9. 2 less than a number, divided by 3

10. 3 more than the product of 10 and a number

11. 5 times the sum of a number and 1

12. The sum of a number and 5, divided by 2

In 13–24, translate the sentence into an equation or an inequality.

13. Seven more than a number, x, is 10.

14. The sum of a number, y, and 6 is 13.

15. Eight more than a number, y, is greater than or equal to 10.

16. The difference of a number, a, and 2 is 8.

17. Six less than a number, z, is less than 21.

18. Thirteen minus a number, b, is 2.

19. The product of 11 and a number, x, is 22.

20. Fourteen is less than 7 times a number, x.

21. A number, a, divided by 2 is greater than 9.

22. The quotient of a number, t, and 3 is 9.

23. Four times a number, b, plus 1 is 17.

24. Three less than the product of 6 and a number, a, is 9.

25. **Geometry** Write an expression that represents the area, A, of the shaded region.

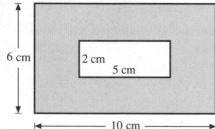

26. **Geometry** Write an expression that represents the area, A, of the given region which consists of a rectangle and a semicircle. (The area of a semicircle is $A = \frac{1}{2}\pi r^2$.)

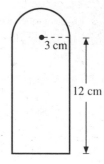

In 27–30, which equation correctly models the situation?

27. **Model Planes** Your model plane collection consists of 15 models. Each plane is either a propeller plane or a jet. There are 7 fewer propeller planes than jets. Let x be the number of jets.

   a. $x + (x - 7) = 15$ b. $x + 7 = 15$

28. **Bake Sale** You want to make 6 dozen cookies for a bake sale. If you follow the recipe, one batch makes 2 dozen cookies. Let b be the number of batches you need to bake.

   a. $2b = 6$ b. $\dfrac{b}{6} = 2$

29. **Height** You are 65 in. tall. You are 18 in. taller than your younger sister. Let h be your sister's height in inches.

   a. $h - 18 = 65$ b. $h + 18 = 65$

30. **Music** An eighth note is played twice as fast as a quarter note. Eight eighth notes can be played in one measure of music. Let q be the number of quarter notes played in one measure of music.

   a. $2q = 8$ b. $\dfrac{q}{2} = 8$

Finishing Homework In 1–6, consider the following question.

Your English paper will be finished once it is typed. The paper is 1200 words long and you type 20 words per minute. It is now 3:50 P.M.. Can you finish the paper before the Superbowl begins at 5:00 P.M.?

1. How many minutes before game time?

2. Write a verbal model that relates your typing speed, the time it would take to type the paper, and the length of the paper.

3. Assign labels to your model.

4. Use labels to translate your verbal model into an equation.

5. Use mental math to solve the equation.

6. Can you finish the paper before the kick-off? Explain.

Traveling to a Party In 13–18, consider the following question.

Your whole family is going to a birthday party for your aunt. The party is at her home which is 110 miles away. The party starts at 8 P.M. and you are just leaving at 6:30 P.M.. If your dad drives 55 mph, will you make it to the party on time?

13. How many hours are there before the party begins?

14. Write a verbal model that relates the distance to be traveled, the speed of the car, and the time it will take to arrive at your aunt's house.

15. Assign labels to your model.

16. Use labels to translate your verbal model into an equation.

17. Use mental math to solve the equation.

18. Did your family make it to the party on time? If yes, how early were you? If no, how late were you?

Soccer Camp In 7-12, consider the following question.

The soccer team has raised $500 to go to summer soccer camp. Since the camp costs $800 the team will have a car wash to raise the additional money. If the charge is $4 per car, how many cars need to be washed to earn the extra money?

7. How much money needs to be raised?

8. Write a verbal model that relates the price of a car wash, the number of cars to be washed, and the amount of money needed.

9. Assign labels to your model.

10. Use labels to translate your verbal model into an equation.

11. Use mental math to solve the equation.

12. How many cars need to be washed?

Building a Toolbox In 19–24, consider the following question.

You are building a toolbox for a Father's Day gift. The toolbox should fit on the shelf by your dad's work bench. This shelf is 10 in. deep. The length of the toolbox is 20 in. and the height is 6 in.. In order to have a volume of 960 in.^{3}, how wide should the toolbox be? Will it fit on the shelf?

19. What is the widest the toolbox can be to fit on the shelf?

20. Write a verbal model that relates the length, height, and width of the toolbox, and its volume.

21. Assign labels to your model.

22. Use labels to translate your verbal model into an equation.

23. Use mental math to solve the equation.

24. Will the toolbox fit on the shelf? Explain.

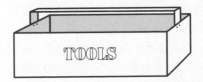

Transportation In 1–3, use the bar graph which shows the means of transportation to school of students at Washington High School in 1990-91.

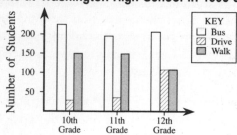

1. Which class has the most students driving to school?

2. Which two classes have the same number of people walking to school?

3. What is the most common form of transportation among 10th graders?

Quiz Grades In 7–10, use the following data which represents the scores that 20 students received on a 10-point quiz.

    10, 8, 4, 6, 7, 8, 8, 9, 6, 7
    1, 7, 10, 7, 8, 6, 8, 8, 7, 9

7. Construct a frequency distribution.

8. Construct a line plot for this data.

9. What was the most common grade?

10. Any score below 6 is an F. How many students failed the quiz?

Chinese Athletes In 15–18, use the bar graph which shows the number of events in which Chinese athletes broke a world record or won a world championship from 1986 to 1989.

15. In which year were the fewest number of world records broken?

16. In which year were the most world championships won?

17. In which year did the number of world championships won decrease?

18. In which year did the number of world records broken remain approximately the same as the previous year?

Pupil-Teacher Ratios In 4–6, use the bar graph which shows the pupil-teacher ratio for public schools in 1966, 1968, and 1970.

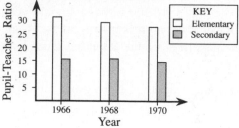

4. Which year had the highest pupil-teacher ratio for elementary school?

5. What was the approximate pupil-teacher ratio for secondary schools in 1968?

6. Which pupil-teacher ratio is decreasing more quickly?

Babysitting Jobs In 11–14, use the following data which represents the number of hours that 20 students spend babysitting during a week.

    3, 7, 2, 4, 4, 4, 0, 3, 2, 3
    0, 2, 3, 5, 5, 7, 6, 4, 3, 3

11. Construct a frequency distribution.

12. Construct a line plot for this data.

13. What was the most common number of hours spent babysitting in a week?

14. How many students did not babysit during the week?

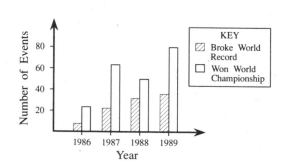

Name _____

In 1–12, graph the numbers on a number line. Then write the numbers in increasing order.

1. 3, 1, 5

2. 0, −2, 4

3. −5, −3, −6

4. 2, −4, 0

5. 2.5, −1.5, −1

6. $\frac{3}{4}$, −$\frac{1}{3}$, 5

7. −$\frac{1}{2}$, −$\frac{3}{4}$, −2

8. 3, −1.2, 5

9. 3.2, 1.5, 5.4

10. −3, 0, 3.1

11. −1, −1.5, −2

12. 4, −3, −1

In 13–18, find the opposite of the number.

13. 5

14. −3

15. 2.1

16. −3.4

17. −17

18. 100

In 19–24, evaluate the expression.

19. $|-8|$

20. $|4|$

21. $\left|-\frac{1}{2}\right|$

22. $|-2.3|$

23. $\left|\frac{3}{4}\right|$

24. $|1.8|$

Profit **In 25–26, use the following information.**

During 1991 the profit earned each month by a small business was recorded in the table below.

Month	Profit	Month	Profit	Month	Profit
Jan.	−$1,250	May	$700	Sept.	$1000
Feb.	−$500	June	$1300	Oct.	$500
March	$0	July	$4000	Nov.	−$200
April	$700	Aug.	$3500	Dec.	−$3000

25. In which month did the business make the most profit?

26. In which month did the busines make the least profit?

Putt-putt **In 27–28, use the following information.**

You and five friends played putt-putt on Saturday afternoon. The winner had the lowest score.

Name	Score	Name	Score
You	−4	Paul	2
Ashley	−1	Kelly	−2
Xue	1	Ashish	−1

27. Who won the game?

28. Who finished last?

Class Enrollment **In 29 and 30, use the following information.**

The table to the right represents the growth in enrollment of the senior class at your high school between 1983 and 1992.

29. Which year showed the largest increase in class size?

30. Which year showed the largest drop in class size?

Year	Increase	Year	Increase
1983	13	1988	−3
1984	21	1989	−10
1985	−11	1990	−18
1986	33	1991	4
1987	7	1992	12

In 1–12, use a number line to find the sum of the numbers.

1. 3 and 5   **2.** 4 and 2   **3.** −4 and 5

4. −6 and 3   **5.** 3 and −5   **6.** 7 and −3

7. −2 and −5   **8.** −4 and −2   **9.** −2 and 2

10. 3, 5, and −6   **11.** −4, 5, and −1   **12.** 3, −10, and 2

In 13–24, use the Addition Rules to find the sum.

13. $4 + 3$ **14.** $-3 + (-5)$ **15.** $6 + (-2)$

16. $-5 + 11$ **17.** $0 + 5$ **18.** $-3 + 0$

19. $-2 + 4 + 6$ **20.** $6 + (-10) + 1$ **21.** $-7 + (-4) + 2$

22. $-1 + (-4) + (-6)$ **23.** $2 + (-5) + 6$ **24.** $4 + (-9) + 5$

In 25–30, simplify the expression.

25. $-4 + 2x + 8$ **26.** $2 + x + (-5)$ **27.** $4x + 1 + (-3)$

28. $3 + 5x + (-3)$ **29.** $2 + 3x + (-3) + 9$ **30.** $5 + (-4) + x + 6$

31. *Mileage* You are picking up a friend and going to a concert. Your friend lives 3 miles west of your house and the concert is 21 miles east of your friend's house. When you are at the concert, how far away from home are you?

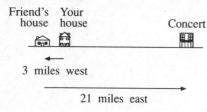

32. *Buffalo Bills* The Buffalo Bills' quarterback was sacked and lost 20 yards on first down. On second down, a 25-yard pass was completed. On third down, the Bills rushed for 6 yards. Did the Bills get a first down (a gain of ten yards)? How many net yards did they gain?

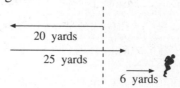

33. *Three-hole Golf* You are playing 3-hole golf. On the first hole you score 1 under par, on the second hole you score 2 over par, and on the third hole you score 1 under par. What was your score for the game?

34. The chart at right represents the profit earned by a company during the first two quarters of the year. Did the company make a net profit? If so, how much?

In 1–12, find the difference.

1. $5 - 3$
2. $7 - 6$
3. $8 - 10$
4. $3 - 11$
5. $-4 - 2$
6. $-7 - 8$
7. $14 - (-2)$
8. $9 - (-3)$
9. $-3 - (-6)$
10. $-5 - (-2)$
11. $4 - |-2|$
12. $-6 - |5|$

In 13–24, evaluate the expression.

13. $2 + 5 - 1$
14. $3 - 5 + 4$
15. $8 - 5 - 6$
16. $-4 + 3 + 6$
17. $-8 + 12 - 5$
18. $-3 - 4 + 12$
19. $-6 - 4 - 2$
20. $-4 - 3 + 2$
21. $-4 + 7 - 2$
22. $6 - (-2) - 4$
23. $-5 + 10 - (-2)$
24. $8 + 3 - (-4)$

In 25–30, evaluate the expression. Then simplify the expression and evaluate the simplified form. Check to see that the two values are equal.

25. $5 - (2 + x)$ when $x = 4$
26. $12 - (-x) - 4$ when $x = 3$
27. $-3 - (x - 4)$ when $x = -2$
28. $8 + (-x) - 5$ when $x = -3$
29. $x - (6 - x) + 2$ when $x = 1$
30. $2 - (6 - 3) + x$ when $x = -4$

31. **Scrabble** You and a friend are playing Scrabble. You use all of your letters first. Your friend must count the points he has left and subtract them from his score. If his score is 148 points when you play and he has 10 points not yet played, what is his final score?

32. **Planets** The distance between the sun and Mars is approximately 141.6 million miles. The distance between the sun and Earth is approximately 92.9 million miles. Approximate the closest distance between Earth and Mars.

33. **Temperature Change** The following table shows the daily high temperatures for a week in May. Determine the change in temperature each day. Find the total of these changes to discover the net change in temperature.

Day	Temperature	Day	Temperature
Sun.	76°	Thurs.	75°
Mon.	72°	Fri.	74°
Tues.	80°	Sat.	78°
Wed.	75°		

34. **Hanging Posters** You want to hang posters around the perimeter of your room. The dimensions of your room are 10 ft by 11 ft. However, you cannot hang a poster over the two windows, the closet, or the door. What is the perimeter of the room available for hanging posters?

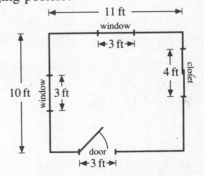

In 1–6, find the sum of the matrices.

1. $\begin{bmatrix} 2 & 3 \\ 4 & 1 \end{bmatrix} + \begin{bmatrix} 5 & 1 \\ 0 & 2 \end{bmatrix}$

2. $\begin{bmatrix} -3 & -5 \\ 7 & -2 \end{bmatrix} + \begin{bmatrix} 2 & 6 \\ -3 & 4 \end{bmatrix}$

3. $\begin{bmatrix} 1 & -3 & 8 \\ -2 & 4 & 6 \end{bmatrix} + \begin{bmatrix} 2 & 5 & -6 \\ 1 & 1 & -11 \end{bmatrix}$

4. $\begin{bmatrix} -5 & 2 & 3 \\ 1 & -4 & 11 \end{bmatrix} + \begin{bmatrix} -2 & 4 & 3 \\ -6 & 1 & -7 \end{bmatrix}$

5. $\begin{bmatrix} 3 & 0 & -2 \\ 0 & -5 & 6 \\ 8 & 2 & -1 \end{bmatrix} + \begin{bmatrix} -8 & 0 & 3 \\ -2 & 4 & 2 \\ 3 & -4 & 6 \end{bmatrix}$

6. $\begin{bmatrix} 11 & 3 & -2 \\ -1 & -5 & -3 \\ 0 & 0 & 4 \end{bmatrix} + \begin{bmatrix} -8 & 4 & 8 \\ 0 & -3 & 0 \\ -2 & 6 & -3 \end{bmatrix}$

In 7–12, find the difference of the matrices.

7. $\begin{bmatrix} 3 & 4 \\ 7 & 1 \end{bmatrix} - \begin{bmatrix} 5 & 3 \\ 10 & 0 \end{bmatrix}$

8. $\begin{bmatrix} -4 & 3 \\ 8 & -6 \end{bmatrix} - \begin{bmatrix} -5 & 2 \\ 1 & -3 \end{bmatrix}$

9. $\begin{bmatrix} 1 & 2 & -3 \\ -8 & 0 & 4 \end{bmatrix} - \begin{bmatrix} 3 & 2 & -6 \\ 3 & 5 & 8 \end{bmatrix}$

10. $\begin{bmatrix} -3 & -8 & 4 \\ 6 & -7 & 9 \end{bmatrix} - \begin{bmatrix} -5 & 2 & 1 \\ 0 & -2 & -1 \end{bmatrix}$

11. $\begin{bmatrix} 3 & 2 & 0 \\ -1 & 0 & 3 \\ 2 & 8 & -4 \end{bmatrix} - \begin{bmatrix} 3 & 6 & 0 \\ 4 & -5 & -2 \\ 9 & -8 & 4 \end{bmatrix}$

12. $\begin{bmatrix} 0 & 2 & -6 \\ 4 & 12 & 8 \\ -3 & -7 & -14 \end{bmatrix} - \begin{bmatrix} -3 & 6 & 2 \\ 11 & -4 & -1 \\ 7 & 6 & -5 \end{bmatrix}$

Pet Store **In 13–15, use the following.**

A pet store currently has German shepherd, Husky, and Lab puppies of both sexes. The table below shows how many of each type are available.

	Male	Female
German shepherd	3	2
Husky	1	0
Lab	2	5

13. Write this table as a matrix.

14. How many male puppies are available?

15. How many German shepherds are available?

Marching Band **In 16–18, use the following.** The table below shows the number of 10th, 11th, and 12th grade students who play a woodwind, brass, or percussion instrument in the marching band.

	Woodwind	Brass	Percussion
*10*th	7	10	2
*11*th	16	7	2
*12*th	14	19	5

16. Write this table as a matrix.

17. How many people play percussion?

18. How many 12th grade students play in the marching band?

19. *Volleyball Camp*   A local collegiate volleyball team has invited the varsity and junior varsity squads of four schools to attend its annual volleyball camp. Find the numbers of 11th and 12th grade students each school will bring.

Number of Varsity Players	10th	11th	12th
Grant H.S.	0	4	10
Lincoln H.S.	1	6	3
Monroe H.S.	1	6	5
Adams H.S.	0	5	8

Number of JV Players	10th	11th	12th
Grant H.S.	7	5	0
Lincoln H.S.	6	6	1
Monroe H.S.	7	4	1
Adams H.S.	5	4	2

In 1–12, find the product.

1. $(-3)(2)$

2. $4(-5)$

3. $(-4)(-3)$

4. $(-2x)(4)$

5. $(5x)(-3)$

6. $6(-3x)$

7. $(-2)^3$

8. $(-3x)^2$

9. $(-3)(x^2)$

10. $(-3)(x)(7)$

11. $(-2x)(-4)(x)$

12. $(-3)(-2x)(-4)$

In 13–24, evaluate the expression.

13. $3x^2 + 2x$ when $x = -2$

14. $-4x + x$, when $x = 4$

15. $x - 2x$, when $x = -5$

16. $4x - x^2$, when $x = 3$

17. $4x^2 + 5x$, when $x = -1$

18. $-3x - 4x$, when $x = -2$

19. $7x + x$, when $x = -3$

20. $2x^2 - 5x$, when $x = 2$

21. $x^3 + 4x^2$, when $x = -3$

22. $5x - (-2x^3)$, when $x = 1$

23. $|12 - x| - 2x$, when $x = 5$

24. $-2x^2 + 3x - 4$, when $x = 2$

25. *Bike Tire* There is a slow leak in your bike tire. It is losing air at a rate of 2 pounds per square inch per day. Let x represent the amount of air in the tire now. Write an expression for the amount of air in the tire after 3 days. If the amount of air in the tire is now 75 pounds per square inch, find the amount of air in the tire after 3 days.

26. *Draining Water* Water is being drained out of a tank at a rate of 10 cubic feet per minute. Let W represent the amount of water in the tank now. Write an expression for the amount of water in the tank after 7 minutes. If the amount of water in the tank is now 1000 cubic feet, find the amount of water in the tank after 7 minutes.

27. *Auditorium Capacity* The seating in an auditorium is divided into five sections. The total number of seats is 2000. The two center sections each have 600 seats. The outside sections each have 200 seats. Which of the following correctly describes the number of seats available in the balcony?

a. $2(600) + 2(200) - 2000$

b. $2000 - [2(600) + 2(200)]$

How many seats are in the balcony?

28. *Cheerleading* During a cheer at half-time, the cheerleaders form a pyramid. Each level of the pyramid has one less person than the level below. The bottom level has 3 people. Which of the following correctly describes the total number of cheerleaders in the pyramid?

a. $3 + (3 - 1) + (3 - 2(1))$

b. $3 + (3 - 1) + 2(3 - 1)$

How many cheerleaders are in the pyramid?

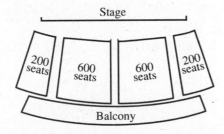

Name _____

In 1–12, apply the Distributive Property.

1. $3(x + 2)$

2. $(x + 5)4$

3. $7(3 - x)$

4. $-6(x + 4)$

5. $-3(8 - x)$

6. $(x - 5)(-2)$

7. $x(5 - x)$

8. $(3 + x)x$

9. $8(4x - 2)$

10. $x(2x - 1)$

11. $(3x + 2)(-x)$

12. $(6x - 1)(-4x)$

In 13–24, simplify the expression.

13. $-3 + x + 7$

14. $x + 7 + x$

15. $3x^2 - 5 + 4x^2$

16. $8x + 3 - 4x$

17. $2(2x + 1) - 5$

18. $3(2x - 4) - 8x$

19. $10x + (3x + 2)(-2)$

20. $2x(3 - x) + x^2$

21. $x(x - 6) + 8x$

22. $-12x^2 + (3x - 1)(5x)$

23. $x^2 - (3 + x^2)$

24. $(-3x)(x - 1) + x^2$

25. **Geometry** Write an expression for the perimeter of the triangle shown below.

26. **Geometry** Write an expression for the perimeter of the trapezoid shown below.

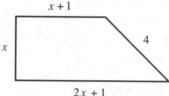

27. **Geometry** Find the area of the shaded rectangle in two different ways. Show how the results are related to the Distributive Property.

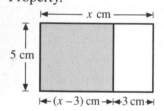

28. **Weight Lifting** A weight lifter puts an x-lb weight on each side of a bar. A weight 5 lbs heavier than the first is then added to both sides. Finally, a weight 5 lbs heavier than the second weight is added to both sides. The expression $2[x + (x + 5) + (x + 2(5))]$ models the total weight lifted. Simplify the expression. What would the expression be if each added weight was 10 lbs heavier than the previous weight?

29. **Play Ticket Sales** You are selling $3 tickets for the school play. For Friday's performance, 100 tickets were sold. Let T be the number of tickets sold for Saturday's performance. Which equations correctly model the revenue, R, earned?

a. $R = 3(T + 100)$

b. $T = 3(R - 100)$

c. $R = 3T + 100$

d. $R = T + 300$

e. $R = 3T + 300$

f. $T = 3R - 300$

30. **Interest Earned** You put $100 in a savings account which pays an annual interest rate of 4% for 2 years. Which equations correctly model the interest earned, I, if you kept the money in the account an additional t years?

a. $I = 100 \cdot 0.04(t - 2)$

b. $I = 100 \cdot 0.04(2 + t)$

c. $I = 100t + 200$

d. $I = 100 \cdot 0.04t - 100 \cdot 2$

e. $I = 100(t + 2)$

f. $I = 100 \cdot 0.04 \cdot 2 + 100 \cdot 0.04t$

In 1–12, perform the indicated division.

1. $18 \div 9$

2. $24 \div 3$

3. $6 \div \frac{1}{2}$

4. $7 \div \frac{1}{3}$

5. $\frac{5}{\frac{1}{4}}$

6. $\frac{16}{\frac{4}{3}}$

7. $-30 \div 3$

8. $12 \div -4$

9. $5 \div -\frac{1}{3}$

10. $-\frac{2}{3} \div \frac{1}{5}$

11. $-\frac{1}{7} \div -4$

12. $\frac{x}{4} \div -3$

In 13–24, evaluate the expression.

13. $\frac{x+2}{y}$, when $x = 8$ and $y = 2$

14. $\frac{x-y}{4}$, when $x = 17$ and $y = 1$

15. $\frac{x-y}{7}$, when $x = 1$ and $y = 15$

16. $\frac{10-x}{y}$, when $x = 8$ and $y = \frac{1}{3}$

17. $\frac{4+x}{y}$, when $x = -4$ and $y = 2$

18. $\frac{3x-2}{y}$, when $x = 6$ and $y = 8$

19. $\frac{4x-3}{y}$, when $x = 3$ and $y = -3$

20. $\frac{5x+2}{y}$, when $x = -2$ and $y = -4$

21. $\frac{2x+1}{y}$, when $x = -5$ and $y = \frac{1}{2}$

22. $\frac{x}{3y+4}$, when $x = \frac{1}{2}$ and $y = -2$

23. $\frac{3x+2y}{x}$, when $x = 2$ and $y = -2$

24. $\frac{xy}{x-y}$, when $x = -10$ and $y = -6$

25. **Parking Meter** One quarter will give 40 minutes at a parking meter. If you will be gone 2 hours (or 120 minutes), how many quarters do you need to deposit?

26. **Musical Notes** A musical note C, one octave above middle C, has a period of $\frac{1}{550}$ second. What is the frequency reciprocal of the period of this note?

27. **Cookies** Your mom agreed to make cookies for the Spanish Club bake sale. Half of the cookies she made are for the bake sale and half are for a care package for your sister in college. Your sister has two roommates. Your sister and her roommates divide the cookies evenly. If your mom made 72 cookies, how many do they each get?

28. **Yearbook Ads** You are in charge of the lay-out for ads in the back of the yearbook. The area available on one page is 63 square inches. If you put four ads of the same size on one page, how much area does each ad receive?

29. **Sewing** You have 4 yards of 60-inch wide cotton material. If you can make one T-shirt from a 2-foot length of material, how many T-shirts can you make?

30. **Candy Bar** You are going to split a large candy bar with 2 friends. If the length of the candy bar is 6 in., what is the length of each piece after the candy bar is split?

1. **Hourly Wages** You were paid $15 for babysitting 6 hours. What was your hourly rate?

2. **Dance Lessons** You signed up for 20 dance lessons. The total cost for the lessons is $100. What is the cost per lesson?

3. **Price per Acre** Sixteen acres of land is for sale at $10,000. What is the cost per acre?

4. **Average Grade** You scored 328 points on four tests. What was your average score?

5. **Pinball Game** A pinball machine costs $0.75 to play 5 balls. What is the cost of playing one ball? Because of your high score, you get to play a sixth ball. What is the cost per ball now?

6. **Basketball Scoring** During the four periods of a basketball game you scored 8, 12, 2, and 10 points, respectively. Find the average number of points scored per period.

7. **Average Growth** You have grown 6 inches in the past $2\frac{1}{2}$ years. What is your average growth per year?

8. **Pittsburgh Pirates** The Pittsburgh Pirates have won 22 of the 31 games played so far this season. What is their win-loss ratio?

9. **Student-Teacher Ratio** In 1991, the enrollment at a college was 2800. The number of teachers at this institution was 800. What was the student-teacher ratio?

10. **Fumble Recovery** The football team fumbled the ball 18 times during the season. They recovered the ball 12 times. What was their recovery-loss ratio?

11. **Video Games** Video games cost $17 each. The video store is running a special of 2 games for $32.98. What is the cost per game under the special? How much do you save per game?

12. **Bookstore** Your favorite author has published a series of 5 science fiction books. Each book costs $4.75. The bookstore is offering the whole series for $20. What is the cost per book for the series? Which is the better buy?

Day Care In 13 and 14, use the following information.

In selecting a day care center for your little brother, your parents have narrowed the choices to three centers. They will choose the center with the greatest adult-child ratio.

Center	Adults	Children
Sunnyside Center	10	50
Westside Day Care	9	54
Little Ones Day Care	13	52

13. What is the adult-child ratio at each center?

14. Which center will your parents choose?

15. **Volume of a Filing Cabinet** What is the ratio of the volume of a drawer in a filing cabinet to the volume of the entire filing cabinet?

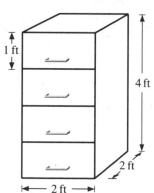

In 1–12, solve the equation by adding or subtracting the same number from both sides.

1. $x + 2 = 14$ **2.** $x - 3 = 6$ **3.** $-1 = x - 4$

4. $x + 8 = 7$ **5.** $13 = 6 + x$ **6.** $x + 4 = -7$

7. $1 = 5 + x$ **8.** $3 = -12 + x$ **9.** $x - 3 = -10$

10. $-10 = -6 + x$ **11.** $-5 + x = -2$ **12.** $7 + x = 7$

In 13–24, solve the equation by multiplying or dividing by the same number.

13. $4x = 12$ **14.** $-5x = 40$ **15.** $-32 = 16x$

16. $-3x = -18$ **17.** $5 = \frac{1}{4}x$ **18.** $-6 = \frac{3}{4}n$

19. $3 = -9x$ **20.** $-x = \frac{1}{2}$ **21.** $7 = 35x$

22. $-\frac{1}{2}x = -6$ **23.** $\frac{x}{3} = \frac{1}{6}$ **24.** $\frac{x}{-3} = 1$

Similar Triangles In 25 and 26, the two triangles are similar. Find the length of the side marked x.

25.

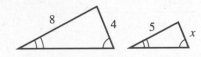

26.

27. *Dimensions of a Banner* You are working on a banner for Friday's pep rally. The length of the banner is 4 times the width. The length is 12 feet. What is the width?

28. *Running Laps* In gym class you have to run $1\frac{1}{2}$ miles on the track. One lap is $\frac{1}{4}$ mile. How many laps do you need to run?

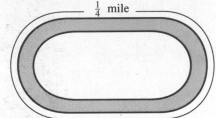

29. *Distance Between Two Cities* It takes 7 hours to fly from City A to City B. After a stop at City B, you fly on to City C. The total flight time is 15 hours. How long did it take to fly from City B to City C?

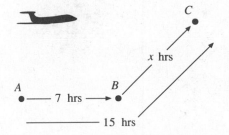

In 1–12, solve the equation by using two or more transformations.

1. $2x + 3 = 11$

2. $3x - 1 = 8$

3. $5 = 5x - 20$

4. $\frac{1}{2}x + 3 = -4$

5. $6 = \frac{1}{3}x + 4$

6. $-2 = 2x + 5$

7. $-3 + 7x = -17$

8. $2 - 4x = 18$

9. $\frac{5}{2} = \frac{3}{2} - x$

10. $-\frac{1}{2}x + 7 = 1$

11. $8 = 4 + 2x$

12. $\frac{2}{3}x - \frac{2}{3} = 0$

In 13–24, solve the equation by simplifying both sides and then using transformations to isolate the variable.

13. $2x + 3x = 5$

14. $10x - 3x = 20 + 1$

15. $\frac{1}{4}x - x = -15$

16. $3x + 2(x + 5) = 0$

17. $2(x - 4) = 2$

18. $\frac{1}{3}(x + 6) = 1$

19. $10 = \frac{1}{2}(4x + 8)$

20. $2(x - 1) + 3(2x + 1) = -7$

21. $4 = \frac{2}{3}x + 9 + \frac{1}{3}x$

22. $5x + 4 - 8x = 13$

23. $2 - 3(2 - x) = 8$

24. $17 = 2(2x + 9)$

25. **Piano Keyboard** The keyboard of a piano has seven full octaves plus two extra white keys and one extra black key. There are 36 black keys on a piano. How many black keys are there in one octave?

Part of a keyboard

26. **Band Fund Raiser** Your school band needs to buy new percussion equipment. The equipment will cost $2000. You have collected $800 in previous fund raisers. If you sell hoagies at $4 each, how many hoagies will you need to sell to raise the remaining funds?

| Cost per hoagie | · | Number of hoagies sold | + | Money already raised | = | Cost of equipment |

27. **Basketball Court Dimensions** A basketball court is 50-feet wide. The key is 16 feet wide. What is the distance from a sideline to the key?

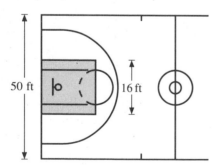

50 ft   16 ft

28. **Wrapping a Package** It takes 64 inches of ribbon to make a bow and wrap the ribbon around a box. The bow takes 30 inches of ribbon. The width of the box is 12 inches. What is the height of the box?

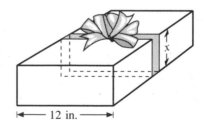

12 in.

In 1–24, solve the equation by collecting like variables on the same side.

1. $2x + 5 = 3x$
2. $-2x = -4x + 20$
3. $7x - 20 = -3x$
4. $7x = 4x - 9$
5. $-8x - 70 = 2x$
6. $\frac{1}{4}x + 3 = -\frac{1}{4}x$
7. $8x - 3 = 2x$
8. $\frac{1}{3}x = 7 - \frac{2}{3}x$
9. $2x + 3 = 4x + 5$
10. $-3x - 4 = 4x + 10$
11. $7x - 3 = 19 + 5x$
12. $6 - 2x = 5 - 7x$
13. $5x + 4 = 2x + 28$
14. $3(x - 3) = 5x - 11$
15. $2(3x + 4) = 5x + 8$
16. $2x + 23 = 3(2x + 1)$
17. $4(x + 2) = -4 - 2x$
18. $5x = 5(-3 + 2x)$
19. $\frac{1}{2}(2x - 6) = 2x$
20. $12x + 44 = x$
21. $3(4 + x) = 2(x - 1)$
22. $2x = 10x + 16$
23. $-3x - 54 = -12x$
24. $2(3 - x) = 22 + 2x$

25. **Dimensions of a Circular Flower Garden** A flower garden has the shape pictured below. The diameter of the outer circle is twice the diameter of the inner circle. The lengths of the walkways are each 6 feet long. What is the diameter of the inner circle?

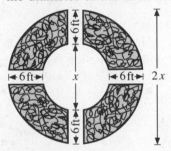

26. **Balanced Scale** On one side of a scale there are 6 coins, 3 weighing 2 grams each and 3 weighing x grams each. The scale is balanced if 5 coins weighing x grams each are placed on the other side of the scale. How much does each of the unknown coins weigh?

27. **Distance-Rate-Time** Two cars travel the same distance. The first car travels at a rate of 40 mph and reaches its destination in t hours. The second car travels at a rate of 55 mph and reaches its destination 3 hours earlier than the first car. How long does it take for the first car to reach its destination?

$$\boxed{\text{Rate Car 1}} \cdot \boxed{\text{Time Car 1}} = \boxed{\text{Rate Car 2}} \cdot \boxed{\text{Time Car 2}}$$

28. **Teeter-Totter** Two children weighing 40 pounds and 50 pounds are on a teeter-totter, as shown at the right. The 50-pound child is sitting 1 foot closer to the center than the 40-pound child. To balance the teeter-totter, the 40-pound child must sit x feet from the center where x is a solution of the equation $50(x - 1) = 40x$. Solve for x.

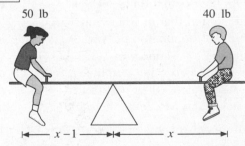

Yearbook Layout In 1–3, use the following.

A page of a school yearbook is $8\frac{1}{2}$ inches by 11 inches. The left and right margins are 1 inch and $2\frac{1}{2}$ inches, respectively. The space between two pictures is $\frac{1}{4}$ inch. How wide should each picture be to fit 3 across the page?

1. Write a verbal model for this problem.

2. Write an equation for the model.

3. Solve the equation and answer the question.

House Design In 4–6, use the following.

You are designing a house with 3 windows, each 3 feet wide, as shown below. There are 4 feet between each end window and an edge of the house. The width of the house is 33 feet. How far apart should the windows be?

4. Write a verbal model for this problem.

5. Write an equation for the model.

6. Solve the equation and answer the question.

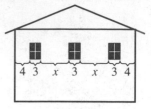

Sewing Flags In 7–9, use the following.

You have volunteered to make flags for the school color guard. Each flag has a red stripe and a 12-inch wide white stripe. The width of each flag is $\frac{3}{4}$ its length. The length is 48 inches. How wide is the red stripe?

7. Write a verbal model for this problem.

8. Write an equation for the model.

9. Solve the equation and answer the question.

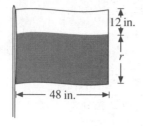

Cassette Storage In 10–12, use the following.

You have a box that is a good size for your tape collection. Two rows of tapes will fit in the box. The box is 10 inches wide. Each tape is $\frac{5}{8}$ inches wide. How many tapes will fit in the box?

10. Write a verbal model for this problem.

11. Write an equation for the model.

12. Solve the equation and answer the question.

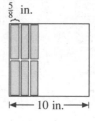

Population In 13–15, use the following.

From 1989 to 1990, the population of Nevada increased by 157,000, and that of Maine increased by 30,000. In 1990, the population of Nevada was 1,206,152, and that of Maine was 1,233,223. If the populations of the two states continue to increase at the same rates, when will the populations of Nevada and Maine be the same?

13. Write a verbal model for this problem.

14. Write an equation for the model.

15. Solve the equation and answer the question.

Population In 16–18, use the following.

From 1988 to 1989, the population of Colorado Springs increased by 5500 and that of Wichita increased by 4700. In 1989, the populations of Colorado Springs and Wichita were 284,482 and 297,391, respectively. If the populations continue to increase at the same rates, when will the populations of the two cities be the same?

16. Write a verbal model for this problem.

17. Write an equation for the model.

18. Solve the equation and answer the question.

In 1–12, solve the equation. Round the result to two decimal places.

1. $3x + 18 = 26$
2. $7x - 1 = 8$
3. $-2 + 4x = 13$
4. $17 = 18 - 6x$
5. $8x - 3 = -24$
6. $39 = 2 - 3x$
7. $-5x + 21 = 80$
8. $21x + 3 = 121$
9. $14(3 - 7x) = 9$
10. $12(2x - 11) = 3x + 43$
11. $-x = 5(-6 - 7x)$
12. $2(x - 3) = 5x + 7$

In 13–24, solve the equation. Round the result to two decimal places.

13. $2.3x + 4.8 = 9.3$
14. $5.1x - 7.2 = 1.4$
15. $7.8 - 6.4x = 8.8$
16. $1.85 = 3.02 + 2.51x$
17. $-5.89x + 7.5 = 2.18$
18. $2.38x + 6.8 = 3.94x - 3.44$
19. $4.91 - 10.27x = 4.11x + 17.56$
20. $.01x = 2(.78 + .03x)$
21. $-3(2.47x + 1.23) = 9.82$
22. $1.32(4x - 3) = 2.38x - 1.52$
23. $3.798x + 12.001 = 5.176x - 3.102$
24. $2.387x + 20.719 = 13.791 - 3.823x$

25. **Purchase of Bike** You are saving money for the purchase of a new bike. You have saved $78.23. The bike costs $152.95. How much more money do you need?

$$\boxed{\text{Money saved}} + \boxed{\text{Money needed}} = \boxed{\text{Price of bike}}$$

26. **Track Meet** The winner of the track meet had an average speed of 5 meters per second. The second-place runner had an average speed of 4.5 meters per second. If the winner finished 2.2 seconds ahead of the second place runner, how long did it take the winner to cross the finish line?

$$\boxed{\text{Rate of winner}} \cdot \boxed{\text{Time } (t)} = \boxed{\text{Rate of 2nd place runner}} \cdot \boxed{\text{Time } (t + 2.2)}$$

27. **Cutting a Rope** A rope which is 10.3 cm long is cut into 4 pieces of equal length. What is the length of each piece?

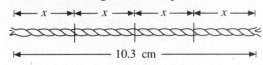

28. **Similar Triangles** The two triangles pictured below are similar. Find the length of the side marked x.

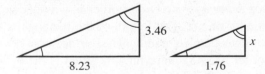

In 1–12, solve for the indicated variable.

1. **Area of a Rectangle**
   Solve for W: $A = LW$

2. **Circumference of a Circle**
   Solve for r: $C = 2\pi r$

3. **Volume of a Circular Cone**
   Solve for h: $V = \frac{1}{3}\pi r^2 h$

4. **Perimeter of a Square**
   Solve for s: $P = 4s$

5. **Distance - Rate - Time**
   Solve for r: $d = rt$

6. **Ohm's Law**
   Solve for R: $E = IR$

7. **Temperature Conversion**
   Solve for C: $F = \frac{9}{5}C + 32$

8. **Profit - Revenue - Cost**
   Solve for C: $P = R - C$

9. **Perimeter of an Equilateral Triangle**
   Solve for s: $P = 3s$

10. **Surface Area of a Rectangular Prism**
    Solve for L: $S = 2WL + 2LH + 2WH$

11. **Angular Velocity**
    Solve for v: $w = \dfrac{v}{r}$

12. **Arc Length** (θ *is a Greek letter*)
    Solve for r: $S = \theta r$

13. **Area of a Football Field** The length of a football field is 360 feet. The area of the field is 57,600 square feet. Find the width of the football field.

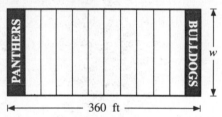

14. **Dimensions of a Paper Cup** The volume of a paper cup, shaped like a circular cone, is 30π cubic centimeters. The radius of the top of the cup is 3 cm. What is the height of the cup?

15. **Garden Fence** You want to put a fence around your vegetable garden. The garden has a square shape. You want the fence to be 1 yard away from each side of the garden. You used 56 yards of fencing. What are the dimensions of your garden?

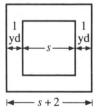

16. **Carpeting** You and your brother are getting new carpet in your bedrooms. The widths of both rooms are 10 feet. The length of your room is $1\frac{1}{2}$ times the length of your brother's room. There are 250 square feet of new carpet. What is the length of your brother's room?

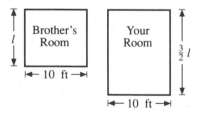

17. **Surface Area** A 5-in. wide border is wrapped around a rectangular prism. The length of the rectangular prism is 8 in. longer than its width. The surface area covered by the border is 340 square inches. What is the width of the rectangular prism?

In 1–3, write the ordered pairs that correspond to the points labeled *A*, *B*, *C*, and *D* in the coordinate plane.

1.
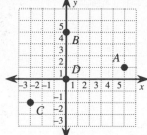

2.
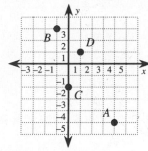

3.
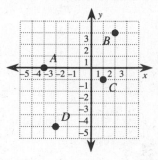

In 4–9, plot the ordered pairs on a coordinate plane.

4. (3, 6), (−2, 5), (2, 2)

5. (−3, −3), (2, −5), (1, 0)

6. (3, −1), (−4, −1), (−1, 6)

7. (5, 2), (−5, 0), (−3, 2)

8. (0, 3), (4, −4), (−2, −4)

9. (−1, 1), (0, −1), (4, 2)

10. *Inches to Centimeters* The table shows some measurements in inches and the corresponding measurement in centimeters. Make a scatter plot for this table. Let each ordered pair have the form (i, c).

i	1	5	10	15	20
c	2.54	12.7	25.4	38.1	50.8

11. *Division Rank* The table shows the division rank of the Cincinnati Reds from 1918 through 1928. Make a scatter plot for this table. Let each ordered pair have the form (t, r) where t is the year (let $t = 0$ represent 1918) and r is the rank. In what year did the greatest improvement occur?

Year	1918	1919	1920	1921	1922	1923	1924	1925	1926	1927	1928
Rank	3	1	3	6	2	2	4	3	2	5	5

12. *Profit* The profit, P (in thousands of dollars), of a small sporting goods store for each month is shown in the table below. January is represented by $t = 1$. Make a scatter plot to represent the data and describe the profit earned over the year.

Month, t	1	2	3	4	5	6	7	8	9	10	11	12
Profit, P (in $1000's)	3	2	2	3	4	7	8	7	5	3	3	7

13. *Quiz Grades* The following table shows various quiz grades for an algebra class and how many students received each grade. Make a scatter plot for the table.

Grade	0	1	2	3	4	5	6	7	8	9	10
Number of Students	0	0	3	1	1	2	8	20	13	9	5

Name _____

In 1–12, sketch the lines on the coordinate plane. Then find the point at which the lines intersect.

1. $x = 3$, $y = 2$　　　　　　2. $x = -2$, $y = 4$　　　　　　3. $x = -1$, $y = -3$

4. $x = 5$, $y = -4$　　　　　5. $x = -4$, $y = 0$　　　　　　6. $x = 0$, $y = 1$

7. $x = 0$, $y = 0$　　　　　　8. $x = 3$, $y = -1$　　　　　　9. $x = 3$, $y = 3$

10. $x = -2$, $y = -6$　　　　11. $x = -1$, $y = -1$　　　　　12. $x = -4$, $y = 1$

In 13–24, write the equations for the horizontal and vertical lines that pass through the given point.

13. $(7, 2)$　　　　　14. $(3, 10)$　　　　　15. $(-6, 4)$　　　　　16. $(-1, 12)$

17. $(3, -2)$　　　　18. $(5, -9)$　　　　　19. $(-11, -4)$　　　　20. $(-4, -7)$

21. $(0, -5)$　　　　22. $(0, 8)$　　　　　　23. $(6, 0)$　　　　　　24. $(-8, 0)$

Babysitting Service In 25–27, use the following information.

You and a friend offer a babysitting service after school. The number of children you watch at any given time is plotted on the graph below.

25. Describe what happened between 4:00 P.M. and 9:00 P.M.

26. Was there ever a time between 4:00 P.M. and 9:00 P.M. when you were not watching any children? If yes, when?

27. How many children did you watch over the longest period of time?

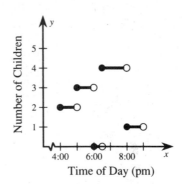

Time of Day (pm)

Honor Roll Ratios In 28 and 29, use the following information.

The following data describes the number of students who were on the honor roll or high honor roll for a certain semester.

Class	Freshman	Sophomore	Junior	Senior
Total Number	215	240	207	228
Honor Roll	43	52	46	44
High Honor Roll	10	12	10	12

28. Find the ratios of the honor roll students to the total number of students for each class. Construct a graph that compares the ratios, y, with the total number of students, x. Describe the results.

29. Find the ratios of the high honor roll students to the total number of students for each class. Construct a graph that compares the ratios, y, with the total number of students, x. Describe the results.

4.2

In 1–12, decide which of the two points lies on the line.

1. $2x + 4y = 8$
   a. $(2, 1)$ **b.** $(1, 2)$

2. $3x - y = 8$
   a. $(2, 2)$ **b.** $(3, 1)$

3. $4y - 3x = 7$
   a. $(3, 3)$ **b.** $(-1, 1)$

4. $-2x - 5y = 6$
   a. $(-3, 0)$ **b.** $(8, 2)$

5. $3y + 4x = -1$
   a. $(-1, -1)$ **b.** $(2, -3)$

6. $5x - 3y = -6$
   a. $(3, 7)$ **b.** $(5, 9)$

7. $y - 4x = -3$
   a. $(-2, -5)$ **b.** $(-1, -7)$

8. $-3y - x = -4$
   a. $(1, -1)$ **b.** $(4, 0)$

9. $2x + y = 0$
   a. $(1, -2)$ **b.** $(-3, -6)$

10. $y = 4x - 2$
   a. $(-1, -6)$ **b.** $(0, 2)$

11. $y = \frac{1}{2}x + 3$
   a. $(-2, 4)$ **b.** $(0, 3)$

12. $y = \frac{1}{3}x - 5$
   a. $(3, -4)$ **b.** $(6, 3)$

In 13–24, use a table of values to sketch the graph of the equation.

13. $y = 2x + 1$

14. $y = 3x - 2$

15. $y = -4x + 2$

16. $y = -x - 3$

17. $y = \frac{1}{2}x + 3$

18. $y = -\frac{1}{4}x + 1$

19. $2x + 3y = 6$

20. $4y - x = 0$

21. $-4x - 2y = 8$

22. $3x - y = 6$

23. $y = 2(x + 1)$

24. $y = -4(2 - x)$

Distance In 25 and 26, use the following information.

Driving toward home at a constant rate of 55 mph, you are 495 miles away. The distance, d in miles, away from home after t hours is given by $d = 495 - 55t$.

25. Sketch the graph of the equation from $t = 0$ to $t = 9$.

26. How far from home are you after 6 hours?

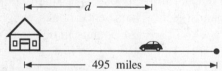

College Account In 27 and 28, use the following information.

The day you were born your grandmother put $500 in an account to help pay your college expenses. Every year, on your birthday, she adds $50 to the account. Not counting the interest earned, the principal in the account may be modeled by $P = 500 + 50t$, where $t = 0$ represents the year you were born.

27. Sketch the graph of the equation from $t = 0$ to $t = 18$.

28. How much principal is in the account at 18 years?

29. **Depreciation** The table lists the value of a car over time. An algebraic model that approximates this data is $y = -2900t + 19,000$ with $t = 0$ corresponding to 1986. Graph the actual data points and the model on the same coordinate plane. Use the model to estimate the value of the car in 1992.

Year	1986	1987	1988	1989	1990	1991	1992
t	0	1	2	3	4	5	6
Value	$20,000	$16,000	$13,500	$10,000	$7,500	$4,500	?

In 1–12, find the x-intercept and y-intercept of the line.

1. $2x + 5y = 10$
2. $3x - 4y = 12$
3. $3y - x = 6$
4. $-2x - 6y = 6$
5. $3x - 8y = -24$
6. $4x + 2y = 16$
7. $9y - x = 18$
8. $-y - 3x = 9$
9. $3x - 2y = 0$
10. $y = 3x - 6$
11. $y = 8x - 4$
12. $y = 6x + 2$

In 13–24, sketch the line. Label the x-intercept and y-intercept on the graph.

13. $y = x + 3$
14. $y = x - 4$
15. $y = 1 - x$
16. $y = -2 - x$
17. $y = 2x + 6$
18. $y = 2x - 4$
19. $y = 9 - 3x$
20. $y = -4x - 8$
21. $3x + 4y = 12$
22. $5y - 3x = 15$
23. $-4x + 8y = -16$
24. $7x - 5y = 35$

Ticket Sales In 25 and 26, use the following information.

You sold tickets to the school play. Advanced tickets were $4. Tickets bought at the door were $5. Total ticket sales were $400.

25. Sketch a graph showing the possible number of people who attended the show.

26. How many tickets were sold at the door if 50 advance tickets were sold?

Club Membership In 27 and 28, use the following information.

The French Club is open to juniors and seniors. There are now 15 members in the club.

27. Sketch a graph showing the possible number of juniors and seniors in the club.

28. How many seniors are in the French Club if 9 members are juniors?

Stacking Crates In 29 and 30, use the following information.

As part of a summer job, you stack crates. The crates have the same length and width, but have heights of 1 or 2 feet. Using a fork lift, you can stack the crates 8 feet high.

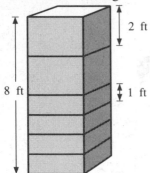

29. Sketch a graph showing the possible number of each type of crate in one stack.

30. If you stacked 3 of the 2-foot crates, how many of the 1-foot crates were in the stack?

Carrying Books In 31 and 32, use the following information.

You help a teacher move books. The math books weigh 3 pounds each. The science books weigh 4 pounds each. You carry 24 pounds in one load.

31. Sketch a graph showing the possible number of math and science books you carried.

32. How many science books did you carry if you carried 8 math books?

In 1–12, sketch the line with the given slope through the given point.

1. $(0, 1)$, $m = 3$
2. $(3, 5)$, $m = -4$
3. $(-1, 2)$, $m = 2$
4. $(-2, -4)$, $m = -1$
5. $(2, 3)$, $m = \frac{1}{2}$
6. $(3, -3)$, $m = \frac{1}{4}$
7. $(2, -1)$, $m = -\frac{1}{3}$
8. $(3, 1)$, $m = 0$
9. $(1, 2)$, $m = -\frac{3}{4}$
10. $(-3, 5)$, $m = -\frac{2}{3}$
11. $(4, 0)$, $m = \frac{2}{5}$
12. $(-2, 1)$, $m = -\frac{5}{8}$

In 13–24, find the slope of the line passing through the given points.

13. $(1, 5)$, $(2, 9)$
14. $(2, 4)$, $(1, 1)$
15. $(4, 1)$, $(2, 7)$
16. $(2, 3)$, $(4, 6)$
17. $(0, 4)$, $(-2, 8)$
18. $(6, -8)$, $(3, 4)$
19. $(3, 7)$, $(-9, -5)$
20. $(-2, 3)$, $(4, -1)$
21. $(-5, 2)$, $(2, -4)$
22. $(3, -1)$, $(-6, 4)$
23. $(-3, -9)$, $(9, -1)$
24. $(-3, -2)$, $(-1, -7)$

25. **Library Books** In 1988 a public library had 16,000 books on its shelves. In 1992 the library had 19,000 books. Find the average rate of change in the number of books per year.

26. **Birth Rate** At Memorial Hospital there were 600 births in 1989. In 1991, there were 550 births. Find the average rate of change in numbers of births per year.

27. **100-Meter Freestyle** In the 1932 Olympics, Yasuji Miyazaki, of Japan, won the 100-meter freestyle in swimming with a time of 58.2 seconds. In the 1988 Olympics, Matt Biondi, of the United States, won the same event with a time of 48.63 seconds. Find the average rate of change in seconds per year.

28. **Postage** In 1989 a postage stamp cost $0.25. In 1992 a postage stamp cost $0.29. Find the average rate of change in postage in cents per year.

Population Growth In 29–32, use the following information.

The table shows the population of Delaware from 1940 to 1990.

Year, t	1940	1950	1960	1970	1980	1990
Population	226,500	318,000	446,300	548,100	594,300	658,000

29. Estimate the average yearly rate of change in population from 1940 to 1990.

30. Estimate the average yearly rate of change in population from 1970 to 1980.

31. Estimate the average yearly rate of change in population from 1980 to 1990.

32. Was the average yearly rate of change in population greater from 1970 to 1980, or from 1980 to 1990?

In 1–6, find the slope and the *y*-intercept of the line.

1. $y = 3x + 2$ 2. $y = 5x - 4$ 3. $y = -2x + 3$

4. $y = 7 - \frac{1}{5}x$ 5. $y = -\frac{1}{3}x - 2$ 6. $2y = x + 4$

In 7–18, write in slope-intercept form. Then sketch the line.

7. $x + y - 5 = 0$ 8. $y - x = 0$ 9. $y + 3x + 2 = 0$

10. $y + 2x - 4 = 0$ 11. $y + 4 = 0$ 12. $y - 2x - 3 = 0$

13. $y - \frac{1}{2}x + 3 = 0$ 14. $2y + 4x - 6 = 0$ 15. $3y - x - 3 = 0$

16. $2x + 6y + 12 = 0$ 17. $-5x - 10y + 10 = 0$ 18. $-2y + x - 4 = 0$

In 19–24, determine whether or not the two lines are parallel.

19. $y = 3x - 2$
$y = \frac{1}{3}x + 4$

20. $y = \frac{1}{4}x - 3$
$y = -\frac{1}{4}x + 8$

21. $2x + y = 3$
$2x + y - 14 = 0$

22. $3y = x - 9$
$3y + x - 3 = 0$

23. $5y - x - 2 = 0$
$2y - 10x + 2 = 0$

24. $3x + 2y = 1$
$-2y = 3x - 2$

Jogging **In 25–27, use the following information.**

Marcos decides to start jogging every day at the track. The first week he jogs 4 laps. He adds 1 lap each week for 8 weeks. Let l represent the number of laps Mario runs and let t represent the time in weeks.

25. Plot points for the number of laps Marcos jogs at one week intervals. Then draw a line through the points.

26. Find the slope of the line. What does it represent?

27. Find the l-intercept of the line. What does it represent?

Movie Rentals **In 28–30, use the following information.**

It costs $10 to become a member at a movie rental store and $2 to rent a movie. Let C represent your total cost for movies for the first month. Let x represent the number of movies you rent.

28. Plot points for your cost if you rent 1, 2, 3, 4, 5, or 6 movies. Then draw a line through the points.

29. Find the slope of the line. What does it represent?

30. Find the C-intercept of the line. What does it represent?

Weight Loss **In 31 and 32, use the following information.**

The graph at right represents the weight loss of a wrestler as he prepares for the state meet.

31. Find the slope of the line. What does it represent?

32. Find the w-intercept. What does it represent?

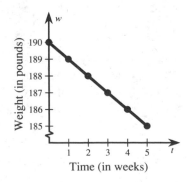

In 1–12, write an equation of a line whose *x*-intercept is the solution of the one-variable equation.

1. $3x + 2 = 7$ **2.** $4x + 12 = 6$ **3.** $7x - 6 = 4$

4. $-2x - 8 = 3$ **5.** $3 + 5x = -6$ **6.** $-7x + 3 = 2$

7. $6 - 11x = 8$ **8.** $4x - 2 = -3$ **9.** $3x - 8 = -5$

10. $-8x + 5 = -2$ **11.** $-6x - 9 = -8$ **12.** $-3 - 10x = -6$

In 13–24, solve the equation. Check your solution algebraically and graphically.

13. $3x + 7 = -2$ **14.** $2x - 3 = 5$ **15.** $4x - 5 = -1$

16. $5x + 11 = 1$ **17.** $-2x - 3 = -7$ **18.** $-4x - 2 = 6$

19. $16 - 3x = 1$ **20.** $-7x + 3 = -4$ **21.** $4 + 6x = 2$

22. $-4x + 3 = 1$ **23.** $8x - 2 = -4$ **24.** $-6x + 4 = -5$

25. *Geometry* The line $y = -x + 25$ represents all possible dimensions of a rectangle with a perimeter of 50 cm, where *x* represents the length and *y* represents the width. According to this model, what is the length of the rectangle if the width is 15 cm? Solve algebraically and graphically.

26. *Geometry* The line $y = -\frac{1}{2}x + \frac{13}{2}$ represents all possible dimensions of an isosceles triangle with a perimeter of 13 in., where *x* represents the base and *y* represents the two equal sides. According to the model, what is the length of the base if the sides are 5 in. each? Solve algebraically and graphically.

27. *High School Alumni* The number of students who graduated from Clairmont High School between 1980 and 1990 is approximately given by $A = 250t + 2000$, where *A* represents the number of alumni and *t* represents the year with $t = 0$ corresponding to 1980. According to the model, in what year were there 3250 alumni? Solve algebraically and graphically.

28. *Record Sales* The number of records sold at a local music store between 1975 and 1990 is approximately given by $y = -350t + 6000$, where *y* represents the number of records sold and *t* represents the year with $t = 0$ corresponding to 1975. According to this model, in what year did the store sell 1100 records? Solve algebraically and graphically.

29. *Interstate 94* Let the *x*-axis of a coordinate plane lie on the southern border of Minnesota and the *y*-axis lie on the western border. Interstate 94 can then be represented by the equation $y = -0.6x + 223$, where *x* is the distance in miles east of the western border and *y* is the distance in miles north of the southern border. If you are traveling on Interstate 94 and are 163 miles north of the southern border, how far east of the western border are you? Solve algebraically.

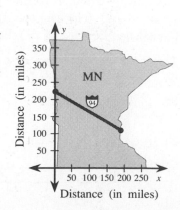

Distance (in miles)

In 1–12, find the coordinates of the vertex of the graph.

1. $y = |x| + 3$
2. $y = |x| - 5$
3. $y = -|x| + 1$
4. $y = |x + 8|$
5. $y = |x - 4|$
6. $y = -5|x + 2|$
7. $y = |x - 3| + 10$
8. $y = |x + 9| - 14$
9. $y = \frac{1}{3}|x - 1| + 2$
10. $y = -3|x - 6| - 3$
11. $y = \frac{1}{2}|x + 4| + 2$
12. $y = -\frac{3}{4}|x + 7| - 1$

In 13–24, sketch the graph of the equations.

13. $y = |x| + 2$
14. $y = |x| - 3$
15. $y = -|x| + 4$
16. $y = |x + 3|$
17. $y = |x - 5|$
18. $y = 4|x - 1|$
19. $y = -2|x + 6|$
20. $y = \frac{1}{3}|x - 2|$
21. $y = |x - 7| + 3$
22. $y = -|x + 1| - 4$
23. $y = \frac{1}{2}|x + 3| - 6$
24. $y = -3|x - 4| + 2$

25. **Flag Design** A coordinate plane has been drawn on a flag. Which set of absolute value equations corresponds to the design on the flag?

   a. $y = \frac{1}{2}|x - 4| + 2$
      $y = -\frac{1}{2}|x - 4| + 2$

   b. $y = 2|x - 4| + 2$
      $y = -2|x - 4| + 2$

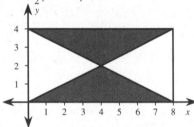

26. **Sewing Stitch** The pattern of a zigzag stitch has been enlarged and a coordinate plane drawn on it. Find the absolute value equations for the 3 indicated graphs.

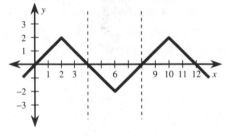

27. **Bounce Pass** While playing basketball, you throw a bounce pass. The ball is 4 feet off the ground when you release it. It bounces on the floor 4 feet in front of you. The receiver of the pass is an additional 3 feet away. The ball follows a path given by $y = |x - 4|$. How high off the ground is the ball when the pass is caught?

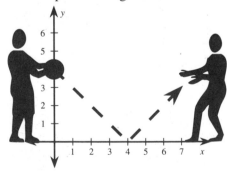

28. **Pool Shot** You are playing pool on an 8-foot by 4-foot table. You try to get the 4 ball into the corner pocket. The cue ball follows the path given by $y = \frac{4}{3}|x - 5|$. Did you sink the shot? (That is, is (8, 4) a solution to the equation?)

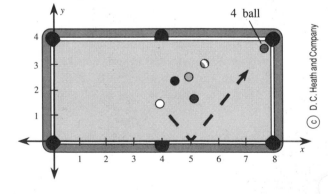

4 ball

In 1–12, solve the equation algebraically.

1. $|x + 2| = 3$

2. $|x - 4| = 1$

3. $|6 - x| = 7$

4. $|x + 1| + 5 = 8$

5. $|4x + 3| - 2 = 0$

6. $|x - 7| - 4 = 3$

7. $|3x - 2| + 4 = 6$

8. $8 - |x + 3| = -15$

9. $\frac{1}{2}|3x + 2| = 7$

10. $2|x + 1| - 6 = 4$

11. $-3|x - 4| + 2 = -7$

12. $2\left|\frac{1}{2}x - 1\right| - 3 = 9$

In 13–24, solve the equation. Use a graphic check.

13. $|x - 7| = 5$

14. $|x + 3| = 7$

15. $|2x - 3| = 9$

16. $3|x + 1| = 6$

17. $\frac{1}{4}|x - 3| = 2$

18. $4 + |x - 8| = 5$

19. $|3x + 1| - 6 = -4$

20. $|5x - 2| + 3 = 11$

21. $2|x - 5| - 4 = -2$

22. $\frac{1}{2}|x + 3| + 2 = 3$

23. $4|2x - 1| - 3 = 9$

24. $\frac{1}{3}|6x + 6| + 5 = 15$

Camera Flash In 25 and 26, use the following information.

The top view of the area illuminated by the flash of a camera can be bounded by the x-axis and the equation $y = \frac{3}{5}|x| - 30$, where x is the width, in feet, of the area illuminated and y is the depth, in feet, of illumination.

25. What is the maximum depth of illumination?

26. What is the maximum width of view of the area of illumination?

Clothesline In 27 and 28, use the following information.

A coordinate plane has been superimposed on a picture of a clothesline post. The braces of the clothesline post can be modeled by the absolute value equation $y = \frac{2}{3}|x| - 1$.

27. Given that the straight part of the post is 5 ft, what is the total height of the clothesline post?

28. How wide is the top of the clothesline post?

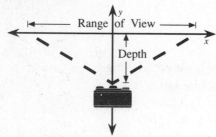

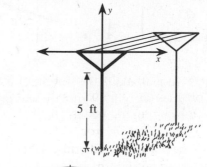

29. *Weighing Meat* You work at a sub shop during the summer. Each sandwich has an average of 3 ounces of meat. However, for speed and ease in measuring, you can vary this amount by 0.5 ounce. What are the minimum and maximum amounts of meat? Find an absolute value equation that models this situation and has the minimum and maximum amounts of meat in a sandwich as solutions.

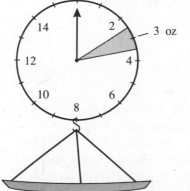

Name _____

In 1–12, write an equation of the line.

1. The slope is 2; the y-intercept is 3.

2. The slope is 5; the y-intercept is 0.

3. The slope is 4; the y-intercept is -3.

4. The slope is -5; the y-intercept is 1.

5. The slope is -3; the y-intercept is -2.

6. The slope is -6; the y-intercept is $-\frac{3}{5}$.

7. The slope is $\frac{1}{2}$; the y-intercept is -8.

8. The slope is $-\frac{3}{4}$; the y-intercept is 9.

9. The slope is $\frac{1}{5}$; the y-intercept is 3.

10. The slope is $-\frac{4}{5}$; the y-intercept is -7.

11. The slope is $\frac{1}{3}$; the y-intercept is $\frac{2}{3}$.

12. The slope is $-\frac{4}{3}$; the y-intercept is $\frac{7}{8}$.

In 13–18, write the equation of the line shown in the graph.

13.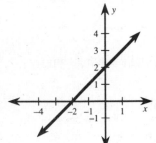

14.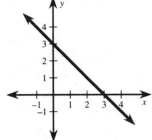

15.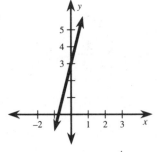

16.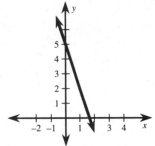

17.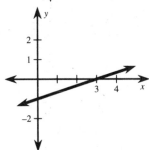

18.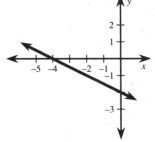

19. **Mammal's Hearts** In mammals, the weight of the heart is approximately 0.5% of the total body weight. Write a linear model that gives the heart weight in terms of the total body weight.

20. Use the equation you found in Exercise 19 to complete the table at the right.

	Human	Cow	Elephant	Whale
Total Weight x, **in lbs**	150	1500	12,000	200,000
Heart Weight y, **in lbs**	?	?	?	?

21. **Photographer's Rate** A photographer charges $50 for a sitting and a basic package of photos. Additional 5 × 7 pictures cost $12 each. Write a linear model that gives the total cost in dollars in terms of how many extra 5 × 7 pictures you purchase.

22. Use the equation you found in Exercise 21 to complete the table below.

Extra 5 X 7 Photos, x	0	1	2	3	4
Cost, y	?	?	?	?	?

In 1–12, write an equation of the line that passes through the point and has the given slope. Write the equation in slope-intercept form.

1. $(2, 4), m = 3$

2. $(3, 5), m = -1$

3. $(-2, 6), m = 4$

4. $(7, -2), m = -3$

5. $(0, -5), m = -\frac{1}{3}$

6. $(-4, 1), m = -\frac{1}{2}$

7. $(0, 8), m = 6$

8. $(-2, -1), m = 5$

9. $(-4, -5), m = -\frac{1}{2}$

10. $(2, 8), m = 0$

11. $(-3, 0), m = 4$

12. $(3, -6), m = \frac{1}{3}$

In 13–18, write the slope-intercept form of the equation of the line.

13.

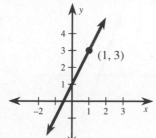

14.

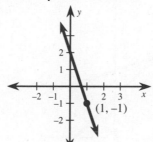

15.

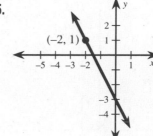

16.

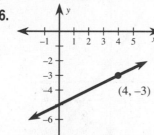

17.

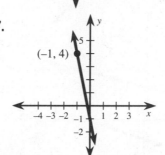

18.

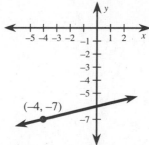

19. *Apartment Rent* Between 1980 and 1990, the monthly rent for a one-bedroom apartment increased by $20 per year. In 1987, the rent was $350 per month. Find an equation that gives the monthly rent in dollars, y, in terms of the year, t. Let $t = 0$ correspond to 1980.

20. *Soccer* During the playoffs you score 2 goals per game. By the end of the second playoff game you had scored 22 goals for the year. Find an equation that gives the total number of goals scored for the year, y, in terms of the number of playoff games, x.

21. *Silkscreening* Your softball team wants to buy new jerseys. To have the name of a team silkscreened on the jersey costs an extra $0.05 per letter. The price of one jersey with the name TIGERS printed on the front is $15.30. Find an equation that represents the price of a jersey, y, in terms of the number of silkscreened letters, x.

22. *Stamp Collection* Between 1985 and 1992, you added approximately 15 stamps per year to your stamp collection. In 1990 you had 130 stamps. Find an equation that represents the number of stamps in your collection, y, in terms of the year, t. Let $t = 0$ correspond to 1985.

In 1–12, write the slope-intercept form of the equation of the line that passes through the two points.

1. $(2, 3), (6, 11)$ **2.** $(4, 2), (3, 5)$ **3.** $(3, -2), (-6, 1)$

4. $(0, 4), (-1, 3)$ **5.** $(-5, -6), (2, 8)$ **6.** $(1, -7), (3, -15)$

7. $(-5, 9), (-2, 0)$ **8.** $(-6, -2), (-10, -14)$ **9.** $(-5, 6), (-6, 1)$

10. $(4, -3), (2, -1)$ **11.** $(-8, 5), (-24, 3)$ **12.** $(-4, -7), (6, -27)$

In 13–18, write the slope-intercept form of the equation of the line.

13.

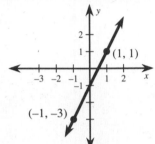

14.

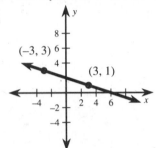

15.

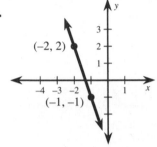

16.

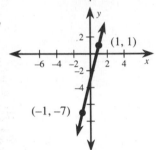

17.

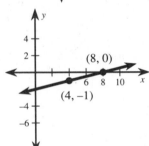

18.

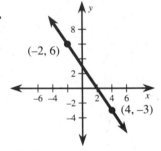

19. *Learning a Language* By the end of your 5th French lesson you have learned 20 vocabulary words. After 10 lessons you know 40 vocabulary words. Write an equation that gives the number of vocabulary words you know, y, in terms of the number of lessons you have had, x.

20. *United Nations* In 1945, when the United Nations was formed, there were 51 members. In 1987, 159 nations were members. Write an equation that gives the number of nations in the U.N., y, in terms of the year, t. Let $t = 0$ correspond to 1945 and assume that membership followed a linear pattern.

21. *Diving* Leslie dives off a block at the edge of the pool. She enters the water 8 ft from the side of the pool. Leslie is 1 ft under water when she is 11 ft from the side of the pool. Write an equation that gives Leslie's depth, y, in terms of her distance from the side.

22. *Nature Hike* Use the diagram at the right to write the equation of the line from point A to point B. What is the slope of this line?

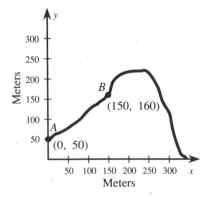

In 1–3, decide whether *x* and *y* suggest a linear relationship.

1.
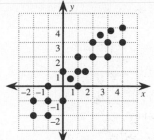

2.
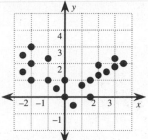

3.
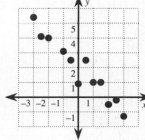

In 4–9, approximate the best-fitting line for the scatter plot.

4.
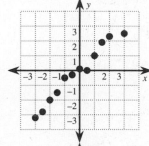

5.
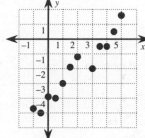

6.
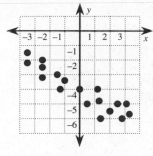

7.
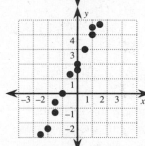

8.
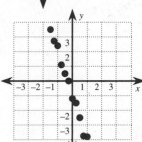

9.
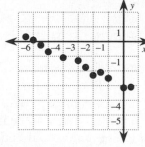

10. *Weight Loss* The scatter plot below shows the weight loss per week of a dieter. In the graph, *y* represents the person's weight in pounds and *x* represents the weeks of the diet. Find an equation of the line that you think best fits this data. Then use the equation to find the dieter's approximate weight after 10 weeks.

11. *Milk Consumption* The table below shows the average number of gallons of milk per week a family drinks. Sketch a scatter plot for this data and find an equation of the line that best fits the data. Then use the equation to find the milk consumption in one week of a 7-member family.

Family Size	Number of Gallons of Milk	Family Size	Number of Gallons of Milk
1	1	4	3.8
2	1.5	5	4.7
3	2.2	6	5

5.5

Name _____

In 1–12, write the equation in standard form with integer coefficients.

1. $2x - y - 8 = 0$ **2.** $6x - 4y + 7 = 0$ **3.** $y = 3x + 2$

4. $y = 5 - 3x$ **5.** $y = -11x - 4$ **6.** $2x = 3y + 5$

7. $y = \frac{1}{4}x + 2$ **8.** $y = -\frac{1}{3}x - 8$ **9.** $y = 4 - \frac{2}{3}x$

10. $y = \frac{1}{5}x - \frac{3}{5}$ **11.** $y = 0.3x - 4$ **12.** $y = -0.6x + 9$

In 13–18, write an equation (in standard form) of the line that passes through the point and has the given slope.

13. $(4, 3)$, $m = 2$ **14.** $(1, 5)$, $m = -4$ **15.** $(0, 6)$, $m = 3$

16. $(-2, 4)$, $m = -6$ **17.** $(6, -8)$, $m = \frac{1}{3}$ **18.** $(-2, 4)$, $m = -\frac{1}{2}$

In 19–24, write an equation (in standard form) of the line that passes through the two points.

19. $(5, 8)$, $(3, 2)$ **20.** $(-2, 5)$, $(3, -10)$ **21.** $(-7, 3)$, $(1, 2)$

22. $(-4, -5)$, $(-2, 5)$ **23.** $(8, 1)$, $(4, -1)$ **24.** $(-6, 6)$, $(3, 3)$

25. *Publicity* You are running for class president. You have $30 to spend on publicity. It costs $2 to make a campaign button and $1 to make a poster. Write an equation that represents the different numbers of buttons, x, and posters, y, you could make.

26. Sketch the line representing the possible combinations of buttons and posters in Exercise 25. Then complete the table and label the points from the table on the graph.

Number of Buttons	0	5	8	10	15
Number of Posters	?	?	?	?	?

27. *Canning Jelly* Your grandmother made 240 oz. of jelly. You have two types of jars. The first holds 10 oz and the second holds 12 oz. Write an equation that represents the different numbers of 10-oz jars, x, and 12 oz jars, y, that will hold all of the jelly.

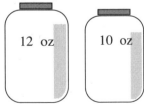

28. Sketch the line representing the possible jar combinations in Exercise 27. Then complete the table and label the points from the table on the graph.

10 oz Jars	0	6	12	18	24
12 oz Jars	?	?	?	?	?

In 1–12, write an equation of the line that passes through the point and has the given slope. Then rewrite the equation in slope-intercept form.

1. $(2, 5), m = 3$

2. $(3, 1), m = -2$

3. $(6, -3), m = -\frac{1}{2}$

4. $(-2, 0), m = -5$

5. $(-4, 3), m = \frac{1}{4}$

6. $(-2, -7), m = -2$

7. $(1, -4), m = 1$

8. $(-3, -2), m = \frac{1}{3}$

9. $(0, 6), m = -\frac{1}{7}$

10. $(4, 4), m = \frac{1}{8}$

11. $(-3, -1), m = -\frac{1}{6}$

12. $(-1, 1), m = \frac{2}{3}$

In 13–18, write an equation of the line.

13.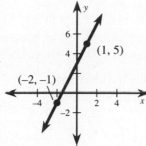

14.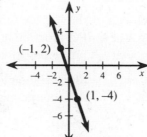

15.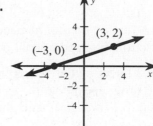

16.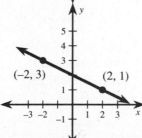

17.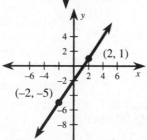

18.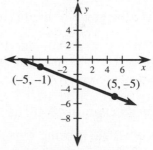

19. Classified Ads It costs $0.75 per day to put a one-line ad in the classifieds. After 5 days, you owe $3.75. Write a linear equation that gives the cost in dollars, y, in terms of the number of days, x.

20. Deer A deer is 4 ft in the air when it leaps over a fence. The deer lands 8 ft away from the fence. Write a linear equation that gives the deer's descending height, y, in terms of the deer's distance from the fence, x.

21. WW II Planes A strafing run was a manuver used by WW II pilots. A plane begins firing its machine guns at an altitude of 1000 ft and 500 ft east of a tower. The first bullet hits the ground 2500 ft east of the tower. Write a linear equation that gives the height of the first bullet, y, in terms of its distance from the tower, x.

22. Running Laps The wrestling team runs 10 laps at the beginning of each practice. For every minute a team member is late for practice, he must run additional laps. Chen was 5 minutes late for practice and had to run a total of 20 laps. Write a linear equation that gives the number of laps run, y, in terms of the number of minutes late for practice, x.

Commission In 1–6, use the following information.

A salesperson earns $1000 a month plus a 7% commission on every item sold.

1. Write a linear model that gives the salesperson's total monthly pay in dollars, y, in terms of the value, x, of the items sold.

2. Use the model to find the monthly pay if the salesperson sells $14,000 worth of items.

3. Sketch a graph of the linear model.

4. What is the slope of the line? What does it represent?

5. What is the y-intercept of the line? What does it represent?

6. What was the value of the items sold, if the salesperson's monthly pay was $1490?

Quality Control In 7–12, use the following information.

A statistical process control (SPC) system is a method of measuring the number of defects in a product. A quality control manager is starting a new SPC program at a base cost of $25,000. The manager can choose to add an additional personal computer (PC) to a department at a cost of $2000 per department.

7. Write a linear model that gives the total cost of the program in dollars, y, in terms of the number of departments that will add an additional PC, x.

8. Use the model to find the total cost if 5 departments receive an additional PC.

9. Sketch the graph of the linear model.

10. What is the slope of the line? What does it represent?

11. What is the y-intercept of the line? What does it represent?

12. If the program costs $39,000, how many departments will receive an additional PC?

Road Construction In 13–18, use the following information.

An interstate is being repaired. Road barriers have been put up to prevent cars from traveling in the left lane. Some of these barriers are 5 ft long, others are 4 ft long. The barriers are in place for a distance of 1 mile (5280 ft).

13. Write an equation that represents the different number of 5-foot barriers, x, and 4-foot barriers, y, used.

14. How many 4-foot barriers are used if 1000 5-foot barriers are used?

15. How many 5-foot barriers are used if 670 4-foot barriers are used?

16. Write the equation from Exercise 13 in slope-intercept form.

17. What is the slope of the line?

18. What is the y-intercept of the line?

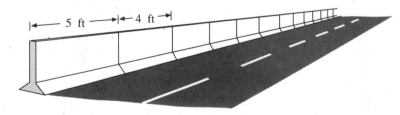

In 1–6, sketch a graph of the inequality.

1. $x < 2$ **2.** $x \geq 3$ **3.** $4 < x$

4. $-1 \geq x$ **5.** $x \geq 6$ **6.** $x < 0$

In 7–24, solve the inequality.

7. $x + 3 < 6$ **8.** $x + 5 \leq 3$ **9.** $x - 4 \leq 7$

10. $x - 6 < -8$ **11.** $x + 7 > 3$ **12.** $x + 3 \geq -6$

13. $6 - 2x < -4$ **14.** $4x + 8 \geq -8$ **15.** $8x + 1 \leq 25$

16. $7x - 30 < 19$ **17.** $-7 - 4x < 13$ **18.** $3x - 1 > 1$

19. $6x + 1 \leq -2$ **20.** $2x + 3 < 6x - 1$ **21.** $3x - 2 \geq 7x - 10$

22. $2x - 14 > 4x + 4$ **23.** $6x + 3 \leq 3(x + 2)$ **24.** $-2(x + 4) > 6x - 4$

25. *Body Temperature* Normal body temperature is 98.6° F. Write an inequality that describes the temperature, T, of people with above normal temperatures. Graph the inequality.

26. *Siblings* Maria is 15 years old. Let A represent the age of Maria's younger brother. Write an inequality for A. Graph the inequality.

27. *Temperature* During a bitter cold week in January, temperatures in Seattle, Washington did not exceed $-10°$ F. Write an inequality that describes the temperature, T, in Seattle. Graph the inequality.

28. *Sales* You want to buy a sweater that costs $42. The sweater might go on sale next week. Write an inequality that describes the price, P, of the sweater next week. Graph the inequality.

29. *Volume* A cubical container has a volume of 1000 cm^3. Let V represent the amount of water in the container. Write an inequality for V. Graph the inequality.

30. *Charities* During 1991, the sophomore class raised $400 for a local charity. In 1992, the sophomore class wants to raise at least as much as 1991's class. Write an inequality that describes the money, m, 1992's sophomore class wants to raise. Graph the inequality.

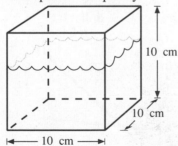

10 cm

10 cm

10 cm

31. *Erosion* A valley is 50 feet above sea level. A stream which flows through the valley slowly erodes the land. Let a represent the valley's altitude above sea level. Write an inequality that describes a over time. Graph the inequality.

Stream →

Sea Level →

50 ft

1. **Dinosaurs** The largest dinosaur, the Brachiosaurus, was 160,000 lbs. Write an inequality to describe the weight of a Stegosaurus.

2. **Rollercoasters** In order to ride the rollercoaster at an amusement park, you must be at least 42 inches tall. Write an inequality to describe the heights of all the people on the rollercoaster.

3. **Grades** The highest grade in your class on the history exam was 94 points. Write an inequality that describes the second highest grade in the class.

4. **Basketball Score** The losing basketball team scored 71 points during the game. Write an inequality that describes the winner's score.

5. **Geometry** For the circumference of a circle to be at least 22π cm, what can the radius, r, be?

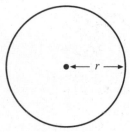

6. **Geometry** For the area of the triangle shown below to be more than 12 in^2, what can the base, x, be?

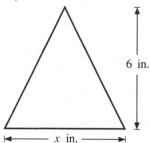

6 in.

x in.

7. **Drink Refills** The price of a glass of lemonade is $1.00 plus $0.25 for each refill. You have $1.65. Use an inequality to find the number of refills you can afford.

8. **Ticket Sales** Tickets for a charity ball were $5 per ticket. Extra donations were also accepted during the ticket sale. Use an inequality to find the possible numbers of tickets sold if $1672 was collected.

9. **Movie and Video Cameras** From 1980 to 1990, the sale of movie cameras per year in a chain of photography shops dropped from 101 to 1, and the sale of video cameras per year rose from 10 to 530. In what year did the sale of video cameras first exceed the sale of movie cameras?

10. **Foreign Currency** From 1980 to 1991 the number of Mexican pesos per U.S. dollar rose from 23 to 2894, and the number of Italian lira per U.S. dollar rose from 856 to 1163. During what year did the number of pesos per U.S. dollar first exceed the number of lira per U.S. dollar?

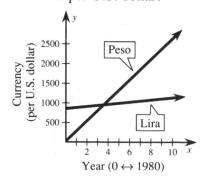

In 1–12, solve the inequality.

1. $1 < x + 3 < 5$

2. $-2 \le x - 4 < 1$

3. $-3 \le 5 - x \le -2$

4. $3 < 2x + 1 < 7$

5. $-1 < 3x - 4 \le 5$

6. $-7 \le 3 - 2x < 13$

7. $-8 < 2x + 4 \le -2$

8. $2 \le 2(x - 3) \le 8$

9. $-6 \le 3 - 2(x + 4) < 3$

10. $4 - 3x \le -8$ or $3x - 1 \le 8$

11. $5x + 1 < -14$ or $6x - 1 > -7$

12. $3 + 2x \ge 15$ or $4x - 2 < 0$

In 13–24, write an inequality for the statement and draw its graph.

13. x is between 5 and 9

14. x is at least -6 and at most 2

15. x is between -4 and -1

16. x is at least -3 and at most 0

17. x is between $\frac{1}{2}$ and 7

18. x is between $-\frac{2}{3}$ and $\frac{1}{3}$

19. x is less than 3 but is at least 1

20. x is less than 6 but is at least -2

21. x is less than -5 but is at least -8

22. x is more than 2 but is at most 10

23. x is more than -3 but is at most -2

24. x is more than 0 but is at most $\frac{1}{2}$

25. *Speed Limit* On Pennsylvania's interstate highway the speed limit is 55 mph. The minimum speed limit is 45 mph. Write a compound inequality that represents the speeds at which you may legally drive.

26. *Coupons* You have $60 and a coupon which allows you to take $10 off any purchase of $50 or more at a department store. Write an inequality that describes the possible retail value of the items you can buy if you use the coupon. Write an inequality that describes the different amounts of money you can spend if you use the coupon.

27. *Radar* A ship uses radar to detect approaching planes. A plane is shown as a blip on the radar. Use the diagram below to write an inequality that describes the distance of the plane from the ship.

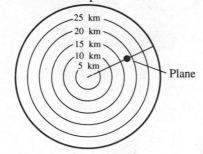

28. *Playing Tennis with a Friend* You live 5 miles from the tennis courts and 2 miles from your friend's house. Write an inequality that describes the distance between the tennis courts and your friend's house. Write an inequality that describes the distance you travel if you go to your friend's house and then to the tennis courts.

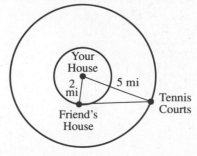

6.4

Name _____

In 1–12, solve the inequality. Then sketch its graph.

1. $|x + 2| < 5$ **2.** $|x + 4| > 9$ **3.** $|x - 3| \le 1$

4. $|x + 7| \ge 1$ **5.** $|4 - x| < 6$ **6.** $|6 - x| \ge 2$

7. $|3x - 6| > 3$ **8.** $|2x + 1| > 5$ **9.** $|2x - 3| \le 7$

10. $|5 - 4x| < 11$ **11.** $|3x + 2| \le 8$ **12.** $|5x + 4| > 0$

In 13–20, write an absolute value inequality to fit the graph.

13.

14.

15.

-7 -6 -5 -4 -3 -2 -1 0 x

16.

0 2 4 6 8 10 x

17.   −5   3

-6 -4 -2 0 2 4 x

18.

-8 -6 -4 -2 0 2 x

19.

-6 -4 -2 0 2 4 6 x

20.

-6 -4 -2 0 2 4 6 x

21. French Horn Range A French horn student has a range of no more than 17 notes from middle C. Let $x = 0$ correspond to middle C. Write an absolute value inequality that shows the range of notes the student is able to play.

22. Shampoo Prices The average price of a particular brand of shampoo is $3.26. Depending on where you shop, the price may vary by as much as $0.25. Write an absolute value inequality describing the possible prices of the shampoo. Solve the inequality.

23. Tool and Die A tool and die shop makes a metal pull tab for a pop can. The length of the tab is 1.2 inches. This measurement may have an error of as much as 0.002 inches. Write an absolute value inequality that shows the range of possible lengths of the tabs. Solve the inequality.

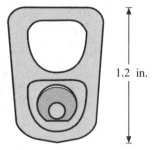

1.2 in.

24. Scale Accuracy To test the accuracy of an industrial scale to 0.01 lb, an object which is known to be 100 lb is placed on the scale. Write an absolute value inequality that shows the measured weight of the object if the scale is **NOT** within accuracy standards. Solve the inequality.

In 1–12, is each ordered pair a solution of the inequality?

1. $x > 4$; (3, 2), (−1, 4)

2. $y \leq 7$; (7, 8), (9, 1)

3. $y - x > 5$; (3, −2), (4, 1)

4. $y + x < -3$; (−1, −5), (0, 0)

5. $y - 2x \leq 6$; (−3, −1), (2, 7)

6. $y + 4x \geq -2$; (1, 3), (0, −2)

7. $3x - y > 4$; (6, 1), (−1, 1)

8. $x - 2y \leq -1$; (3, 1), (4, 2)

9. $2x + 3y \leq 2$; (−3, 1), (5, −2)

10. $4y - 2x > -3$; (−1, 4), (6, 3)

11. $3x - 5y < -2$; (1, 1), (−1, 0)

12. $6y - 7x \geq 3$; (4, 3), (−4, −3)

In 13–24, sketch the graph of the inequality.

13. $x < 2$

14. $y \geq -4$

15. $y - 2x \geq 1$

16. $y + 3x \geq 2$

17. $y + 5x < -6$

18. $y - 3x > -2$

19. $3x - y \geq 2$

20. $7x - y < -3$

21. $2x + 3y \geq 6$

22. $4x - 2y \leq 8$

23. $3x + 5y < -10$

24. $6x - 2y > -4$

25. *Drama Club* The drama club has 40 members. Sophomores, juniors, and seniors may participate in this club. Let x represent the number of sophomores and let y represent the number of juniors in the club. Write and graph an inequality that describes the different number of sophomores and juniors in the drama club.

26. *Calculators* A store carries $3000 worth of various types of calculators. A scientific calculator costs $20 and a graphing calculator costs $80. Let x represent the number of scientific calculators in stock. Let y represent the number of graphing calculators in stock. Write and graph the inequality that describes the different number of scientific and graphing calculators in stock.

27. *Windows* The area of the window shown below is less than 28 square feet. Let x and y represent the height of the triangular and rectangular portions of the window. Write and graph an inequality that describes the different dimensions of the window.

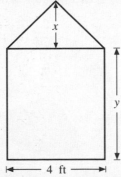

28. *Geometry* The perimeter of a rectangle must be greater than 16 cm. Let x represent the length of the rectangle. Let y represent the width of the rectangle. Write and graph an inequality that describes the different lengths and widths of the rectangle.

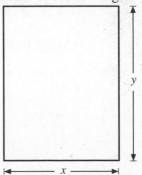

Paul's History In 1–4, use the time line showing a few memorable moments in Paul's life.

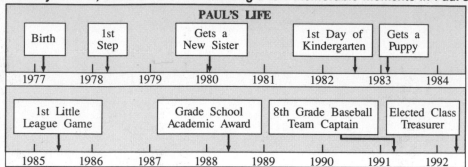

PAUL'S LIFE

| Birth | 1st Step | | Gets a New Sister | | 1st Day of Kindergarten | Gets a Puppy |

| 1977 | 1978 | 1979 | 1980 | 1981 | 1982 | 1983 | 1984 |

| 1st Little League Game | | Grade School Academic Award | 8th Grade Baseball Team Captain | Elected Class Treasurer |

| 1985 | 1986 | 1987 | 1988 | 1989 | 1990 | 1991 | 1992 |

1. What event in Paul's life occurred one year after the United States celebrated its 200th birthday?

2. To what office was Paul elected in 10th grade?

3. Approximately how old was Paul when his sister was born?

4. What special present did Paul receive on his sixth birthday?

Restaurant Prices In 5 and 6, use the picture graph to the right, which compares the average cost of a meal at several restaurants. Each $ represents $5.00.

5. Which restaurant has the most expensive dinners?

6. Which restaurants have the least expensive dinners?

Burger Stop	$
Don's Subs	$
Family Foods	$$
Main St. Pub	$$
Paula's Place	$$$
Piere's	$$$$$$

Spain's GNP In 7–9, use the circle graph showing the gross national product of Spain in 1971. Spain's total GNP was $38,740,000,000. (*Source: World Book Encyclopedia*)

7. What was the value of the agricultural products produced in 1971?

8. What was the value of the industrial goods produced in 1971?

9. How much more was produced in services than agriculture?

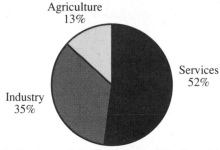

Monthly Budget In 10–12, use the circle graph which shows the monthly budget of a two-person family with a monthly net income of $2000.

10. How much is the couple's monthly rent?

11. How much money is the couple planning on saving each month?

12. How much more money is spent on utilities than food?

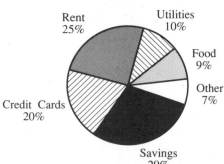

© D. C. Heath and Company

7.1

In 1–6, decide whether the ordered pairs are solutions of the system.

1. $(1, 1)$, $(0, 3)$
$$\begin{cases} 2x + y = 3 \\ x - 2y = -1 \end{cases}$$

2. $(-2, 4)$, $(-1, 0)$
$$\begin{cases} 4x + y = -4 \\ -x - y = 1 \end{cases}$$

3. $(5, 4)$, $(4, 1)$
$$\begin{cases} x - y = 3 \\ 3x - y = 11 \end{cases}$$

4. $(-6, -4)$, $(3, -1)$
$$\begin{cases} x - 3y = 6 \\ 2x - y = -8 \end{cases}$$

5. $(-3, -4)$, $(-1, 4)$
$$\begin{cases} -4x + y = 8 \\ 5x - 3y = -3 \end{cases}$$

6. $(-6, 2)$, $(3, -4)$
$$\begin{cases} -2x - 3y = 6 \\ 3x + 4y = -10 \end{cases}$$

In 7–12, graph and check to solve the system.

7. $\begin{cases} y = -2x + 2 \\ y = x - 1 \end{cases}$

8. $\begin{cases} y = 4x - 2 \\ y = 2x + 4 \end{cases}$

9. $\begin{cases} y = \frac{1}{2}x + 3 \\ y = x + 4 \end{cases}$

10. $\begin{cases} x - 2y = 2 \\ x + 3y = -3 \end{cases}$

11. $\begin{cases} 2x - 3y = -3 \\ 5x - 3y = -12 \end{cases}$

12. $\begin{cases} 3x - 5y = -30 \\ x - 5y = -20 \end{cases}$

13. *Buying Pop* You bought 12 2-liter bottles of regular and diet pop for a school dance. The regular pop was on sale for $1.00 per 2-liter bottle. The diet pop cost $1.50 per 2-liter bottle. You spent $15.00. Assign labels to the verbal model below. How many of each type of pop did you buy?

Number of bottles of regular pop	+	Number of bottles of diet pop	=	Total number of bottles

$1.00	·	Number of bottles of regular pop	+	$1.50	·	Number of bottles of diet pop	=	Total price

14. *Baseball Outs* In a nine-inning game, 18 of a baseball team's 27 outs were fly balls. Fifty percent of the outs made by infielders and 100% of the outs made by outfielders were fly balls. Assign labels to the verbal model below. How many outs were made by the infielders? How many outs were made by the outfielders?

Infielder outs	+	Outfielder outs	=	Total outs

0.5	·	Infielder outs	+	1	·	Outfielder outs	=	Number of fly ball outs

15. *Umbrella Sales* The matrix gives the number of automatic and manual opening umbrellas sold at a shop in 1980 and 1990. Use a linear model to represent the sales of each type of umbrella. Let $t = 0$ correspond to 1980. Sketch the graphs and estimate when the number of automatic umbrellas sold equaled the number of manual umbrellas sold.

	1980	1990
Automatic	10	20
Manual	25	10

In 1–18, use substitution to solve the system.

1. $\begin{cases} y = x + 2 \\ 2x + y = 8 \end{cases}$

2. $\begin{cases} y = x - 1 \\ 2x - y = 0 \end{cases}$

3. $\begin{cases} 2x + y = -3 \\ y = 7 \end{cases}$

4. $\begin{cases} 3x - y = -2 \\ y = 2x + 3 \end{cases}$

5. $\begin{cases} x - 2y = 8 \\ y = -4x + 5 \end{cases}$

6. $\begin{cases} y = -3x - 1 \\ x - 3y = 3 \end{cases}$

7. $\begin{cases} x + y = -3 \\ 3x + y = 3 \end{cases}$

8. $\begin{cases} x - y = 4 \\ x - 2y = 10 \end{cases}$

9. $\begin{cases} 3x + y = 0 \\ x - y = 4 \end{cases}$

10. $\begin{cases} 3x - y = 9 \\ 2x + y = 6 \end{cases}$

11. $\begin{cases} x - 2y = 0 \\ 3x + y = 0 \end{cases}$

12. $\begin{cases} 2x - y = 3 \\ 3x - y = 4 \end{cases}$

13. $\begin{cases} 3x + 2y = 8 \\ x + 4y = -4 \end{cases}$

14. $\begin{cases} x - 5y = -3 \\ 4x - 3y = 5 \end{cases}$

15. $\begin{cases} 2x + 5y = 4 \\ x + 5y = 7 \end{cases}$

16. $\begin{cases} -3x + y = -3 \\ 2x - 5y = -11 \end{cases}$

17. $\begin{cases} 2x - 3y = -14 \\ 3x - y = -7 \end{cases}$

18. $\begin{cases} \frac{1}{2}x + y = 2 \\ 2x + 3y = 9 \end{cases}$

19. **Mowing and Shoveling** Last year you mowed grass or shoveled snow for 10 households. You charged $200 a season to mow a yard and $180 a season to shovel snow. If you earned $1880 last year, how many households did you mow and how many households did you shovel?

20. **Driving** Your mother and father took turns driving on a 580-mile trip that took 10 hours to complete. Your mother drove at a constant speed of 55 mph and your father drove at a constant speed of 60 mph. How long did they each drive?

21. **Room Dimensions** The area of the room pictured below is 140 square feet. The perimeter of the room is 52 feet. Find x and y.

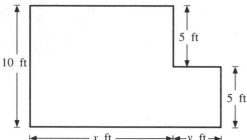

22. **Dimensions of a Triangle** The perimeter of an isosceles triangle is 16 inches. The area of the triangle is 12 square inches. What are the lengths of the sides of the isosceles triangle?

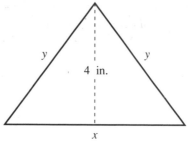

23. **Dimensions of a Metal Sheet** A rectangular hole 2 cm wide and x cm long is cut in a rectangular sheet of metal 5 cm wide and y cm long. The length of the hole is 8 cm less than the length of the metal sheet. After the hole is cut, the area of the remaining metal is 49 cm^2. Find the length of the hole and the length of the metal sheet.

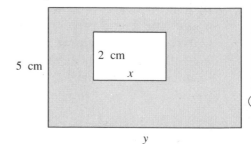

In 1–18, use linear combinations to solve the system.

1. $\begin{cases} x + y = 5 \\ x - y = 7 \end{cases}$

2. $\begin{cases} x - 2y = 8 \\ -x + 3y = -5 \end{cases}$

3. $\begin{cases} x - 4y = 14 \\ -x + 3y = -11 \end{cases}$

4. $\begin{cases} 2x - y = -3 \\ -5x + y = 9 \end{cases}$

5. $\begin{cases} 3x + y = 6 \\ -3x + 4y = 9 \end{cases}$

6. $\begin{cases} 2x - 3y = -16 \\ x + 3y = 10 \end{cases}$

7. $\begin{cases} x - 2y = 9 \\ -3x + 2y = -19 \end{cases}$

8. $\begin{cases} 3x + 4y = 15 \\ -3x + 2y = 21 \end{cases}$

9. $\begin{cases} -3x + 5y = -4 \\ 3x + 4y = 13 \end{cases}$

10. $\begin{cases} -2x + 3y = 14 \\ x - 4y = -12 \end{cases}$

11. $\begin{cases} -x - 5y = 30 \\ 2x - 7y = 25 \end{cases}$

12. $\begin{cases} -x + 8y = 16 \\ 3x + 4y = 36 \end{cases}$

13. $\begin{cases} 2x - y = 16 \\ 3x + 5y = 11 \end{cases}$

14. $\begin{cases} 5x + 2y = 5 \\ 3x + y = 2 \end{cases}$

15. $\begin{cases} 2x + 5y = -22 \\ 4x - 3y = 8 \end{cases}$

16. $\begin{cases} 5x - 4y = -30 \\ 2x + 3y = -12 \end{cases}$

17. $\begin{cases} 4x - 5y = 6 \\ 2x + 3y = -8 \end{cases}$

18. $\begin{cases} -7x + 8y = 32 \\ 5x + 6y = 24 \end{cases}$

19. **Saline Solution** You are making a saline solution in science class. One hundred milliliters of a 50% saline solution is obtained by mixing a 40% saline solution with a 60% saline solution. How much of each must you use?

20. **Concrete Mixture** You are making 10 tons of concrete that is 40% cement by mixing a 20% cement mixture with a 70% cement mixture. How much of each must you use?

21. **Field Goal Kicker** A field goal kicker can kick the football 30 yards into the wind. In identical conditions, kicking with the wind, the ball travels 50 yards. Assign labels to the verbal model. Then solve the resulting system to find the distance the kicker can kick with no wind and the distance controlled by the wind.

| Kicker's distance | + | Wind distance | = | Distance kicked with the wind |
| Kicker's distance | − | Wind distance | = | Distance kicked into the wind |

22. **Pass Play** A wide receiver runs a pattern along the line $y = \frac{1}{2}x$. The quarterback throws a ball that follows the line $y = \frac{1}{4}x + 5$. Find the coordinates of the point where the receiver catches the ball.

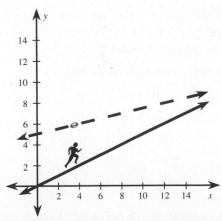

1. **Baseball Glove Sales** A sporting goods store sells right-handed and left-handed baseball gloves. In one month, 12 gloves were sold for a total revenue of $561. Right-handed gloves cost $45 and left-handed gloves cost $52. How many of each type of glove did they sell?

2. **Cookout** You are buying the meat for a cookout. You need to buy 8 packages of meat. A package of hotdogs costs $1.60 and a package of hamburger costs $5.00. If you spend a total of $23.00, how many packages of each can you buy?

3. **Southern Cuisine** Your family goes to a Southern-style restaurant for dinner. There are 6 people in your family. Some people order the chicken dinner for $14 and some order the steak dinner for $17. If the total bill was $99, how many people ordered each dinner?

4. **Dimensions of a Rectangle** The perimeter of the rectangle below is 20 in. The perimeter of the inscribed triangle is 20 in. Find the dimensions of the rectangle.

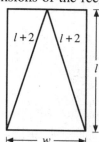

5. **Driving to Grandma's House** You live in Pennsylvania and your grandparents live in Ohio. When you are in Pennslyvania, you drive an average rate of 55 mph. When you are in Ohio, you drive an average rate of 65 mph. The entire trip of 295 miles takes 5 hours. How long does it take to reach the Pennsylvania-Ohio border? How long does it take to get from the border to your grandparents' house?

6. **Election Polls** According to a local survey performed in January, 55% of the people polled said they would reelect the town's mayor. However, the mayor's percentage of votes decreased 2% each month. The survey revealed that 30% of the people polled would vote for the challenger. The challenger's percentage of votes increased 3% each month. In what month will the percentage of people willing to vote for the challenger equal that of the mayor? What percentage will vote for the challenger in that month?

Shipping Costs In 7–10, use the following information.

The flat rate plus the rate per mile that two shipping companies charge to make an 800-pound delivery are listed in the matrix below.

(Dollars)	Flat Rate	Rate/mile
Company A	100	0.30
Company B	200	0.10

7. Find a linear system that describes the cost of shipping with each company.

8. How far must a delivery go for both companies to charge the same amount?

9. Which company is more economical if the delivery is closer than the distance found in Exercise 8?

10. Which company is more economical if the delivery is sent further than the distance found in Exercise 8?

In 1–12, graph the system and describe its solutions.

1. $\begin{cases} x - y = 3 \\ x - y = -2 \end{cases}$

2. $\begin{cases} -3x + y = -1 \\ -3x + y = 2 \end{cases}$

3. $\begin{cases} 3x + y = 1 \\ 6x + 2y = 2 \end{cases}$

4. $\begin{cases} 2x + y = 5 \\ 2x + y = -1 \end{cases}$

5. $\begin{cases} 4x - 3y = 2 \\ 12x - 9y = 6 \end{cases}$

6. $\begin{cases} -x + 2y = -4 \\ -x + 2y = 16 \end{cases}$

7. $\begin{cases} 2x + y = 7 \\ 4x + 2y = -10 \end{cases}$

8. $\begin{cases} -2x + 3y = 18 \\ -2x + 3y = -4 \end{cases}$

9. $\begin{cases} 2x - y = 3 \\ x - \frac{1}{2}y = \frac{3}{2} \end{cases}$

10. $\begin{cases} 3x + 6y = -\frac{1}{2} \\ x + 2y = -\frac{1}{6} \end{cases}$

11. $\begin{cases} 2x - 3y = 3 \\ 4x - 6y = -2 \end{cases}$

12. $\begin{cases} \frac{1}{2}x + y = -\frac{3}{2} \\ \frac{3}{2}x + 3y = 2 \end{cases}$

In 13–15, find a linear system for the graphical model. If only one line is shown, find two different equations for the line.

13.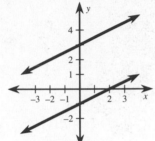

14.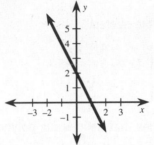

15.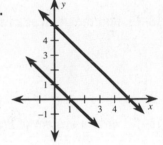

16. *Traveling Time* You pick up your mother at work and then drive to your sister's out-of-town soccer game. Your total trip takes 2 hours to drive 110 miles at an average rate of 55 mph. Can you determine how long it takes to get to your mother's office or how much longer it takes to get to the soccer field from her office? If yes, solve. If not, explain why. Use the verbal model to help answer the question.

| Time from home to mother's office | + | Time from office to soccer field | = | Total trip time |

| 55 | · | Time from home to mother's office | + | 55 | · | Time from office to soccer field | = | Total distance |

17. *Revenue and Cost* The following matrix gives the revenue and cost of running a business from 1987 to 1990. Construct two scatter plots, one for revenue and one for cost. Then find a linear system that describes the revenue and cost. Profit can be defined as revenue minus cost. What does the graph tell you about the business' profit from 1987 to 1990?

(in $1000)	Revenue	Cost
1987	50	25
1988	100	75
1989	150	125
1990	200	175

In 1–12, sketch the graph of the system of linear inequalities.

1. $\begin{cases} y \geq 2 \\ x < -3 \end{cases}$

2. $\begin{cases} y < 2x + 1 \\ y \geq \frac{1}{2}x \end{cases}$

3. $\begin{cases} x + y \geq 4 \\ -3x + y < 1 \end{cases}$

4. $\begin{cases} 2x + 3y < 4 \\ 2x + 3y > -9 \end{cases}$

5. $\begin{cases} 3x - 4y > 2 \\ 3x - y > 2 \end{cases}$

6. $\begin{cases} x \geq 0 \\ y \leq 0 \\ y < x - 2 \end{cases}$

7. $\begin{cases} 2x + y \leq 4 \\ -3x + y < 3 \\ y \geq -4 \end{cases}$

8. $\begin{cases} 4x - y \geq 2 \\ x \leq 3 \\ y \leq 1 \end{cases}$

9. $\begin{cases} -2x + 5y < 5 \\ x + 2y < 3 \\ x < 4 \end{cases}$

10. $\begin{cases} x + 2y \geq 4 \\ y < 5 \\ 3x + y < 5 \end{cases}$

11. $\begin{cases} x < 3 \\ y > -1 \\ x > -2 \\ y < 3 \end{cases}$

12. $\begin{cases} x + y > 3 \\ x + y < 5 \\ -3x + y \leq 0 \\ -x + 2y \geq 0 \end{cases}$

In 13–15, find the vertices of the graph of the system.

13. $\begin{cases} x + y \geq 3 \\ -2x + y \leq 3 \\ 3x + y \leq 13 \end{cases}$

14. $\begin{cases} x + 4y \leq 17 \\ 4x - 5y \leq 5 \\ x \geq 0 \\ y \leq 4 \end{cases}$

15. $\begin{cases} 2x + y \leq 6 \\ 2x + 3y \geq 0 \\ y \leq 4 \\ x \leq 3 \end{cases}$

In 16–17, write a system of linear inequalities that defines the polygon.

16. Rectangle

   $(-1, 5), (-1, -1), (3, -1), (3, 5)$

17. Triangle

   $(-2, 4), (4, 1), (-2, -1)$

18. **Study Time** You need at least 3 hours to do your English and history homework. It is 12:00 P.M. on Sunday and your friend wants you to go to the movies at 7:00 P.M.. Write a system of linear inequalities that shows the number of hours you could spend studying each subject if you go to the movie. Graph your result.

19. **Ordering Cups** You work at a frozen yogurt store during the summer. You need to order 5 oz and 8 oz cups. The storage room will only hold 10 more boxes. A box of 5-oz cups costs $100 and a box of 8-oz cups costs $150. A maximum of $1200 is budgeted for yogurt cups. Write a system of linear inequalities that shows the number of boxes of 5-oz and 8-oz cups that could be bought. Graph your result.

Flag Pattern In 20-22, use the picture of the flag.

20. Write a system of inequalities that defines the red section of the flag.

21. Write a system of inequalities that defines the white section of the flag.

22. Write a system of inequalities that defines the blue section of the flag.

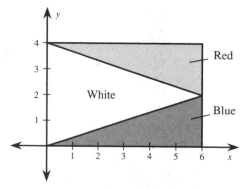

In 1–10, find the minimum and maximum values of the objective quantity, C.

1. $C = 3x + 2y$

Constraints: $\begin{cases} x + y \le 6 \\ -x + y \ge 0 \\ x \ge 0 \end{cases}$

2. $C = 4x + y$

Constraints: $\begin{cases} x - y \ge 0 \\ x + 3y \le 12 \\ y \ge 0 \end{cases}$

3. $C = x + 3y$

Constraints: $\begin{cases} 3x + 2y \ge 16 \\ -x + y \le 8 \\ x \le 4 \end{cases}$

4. $C = 3x + y$

Constraints: $\begin{cases} 3x + 2y \ge 12 \\ -x + y \le 1 \\ x \le 4 \end{cases}$

5. $C = 2x + y$

Constraints: $\begin{cases} x \ge 3 \\ y \le 5 \\ y \ge 0 \\ x \le 6 \end{cases}$

6. $C = x + 4y$

Constraints: $\begin{cases} x + y \le 3 \\ x \ge 0 \\ x \le 1 \\ y \ge 0 \end{cases}$

7. $C = 5x + 3y$

Constraints: $\begin{cases} x + y \le 6 \\ y \ge 0 \\ x \ge 1 \\ x \le 4 \end{cases}$

8. $C = 4x + 2y$

Constraints: $\begin{cases} -x + 2y \le 6 \\ x - y \le 0 \\ x \ge 2 \\ x \le 4 \end{cases}$

9. $C = 2x + 3y$

Constraints: $\begin{cases} x - y \le 5 \\ y \ge 1 \\ x \ge 0 \\ y \le 4 \end{cases}$

10. $C = x + 7y$

Constraints: $\begin{cases} 2x + y \le 4 \\ x + y \ge 1 \\ x \ge 0 \\ y \ge 0 \end{cases}$

11. *Flowers* A florist has to order roses and carnations for Valentine's Day. The florist needs to decide how many dozens of roses and carnations should be ordered to obtain a maximum profit.

- Roses: The florist's cost is $20 per dozen; the profit over cost is $20 per dozen.

- Carnations: The florist's cost is $5 per dozen; the profit over cost is $8.

- The florist can order no more than 60 dozen flowers.

- A minimum of 20 dozen carnations must be ordered.

- The florist cannot order more than $450 worth of roses and carnations.

Use linear programming to find how many dozens of each flower the florist should order.

12. *Land Development* A land developer owns a piece of land surrounding a lake. The developer needs to decide how to divide the land into lots for lake-side homes and regular homes in order to make the maximum profit.

- Lake front home: The developer's cost is $150,000; the profit over cost is $50,000.

- Regular home: The developer's cost is $100,000; the profit over cost is $23,000.

- There is enough land for at most 20 homes.

- There must be a minimum of 10 regular homes.

- The developer can invest no more than $2,200,000.

Use linear programming to find how many lake front and regular homes the developer should build.

In 1–12, simplify, if possible.

1. $3^2 \cdot 3^4$

2. $(2^3)^5$

3. $x^5 \cdot x^3$

4. $(y^2)^8$

5. $(2x)^3$

6. $(-3x^4)^2$

7. $(x^2)^7$

8. $(-2x)^3(-x^2)$

9. $(xy)^3(z^6)^2$

10. $(a^2bc^3)^4 \cdot (b^2c)^3$

11. $(-x)^3(-y^2)^4(xyz^5)^2$

12. $(2x)^3(2y^2)^4 \left(\frac{1}{2}xy\right)^5$

In 13–24, simplify. Then evaluate the expression when $x = 2$ and $y = 1$.

13. $(x^3)^2$

14. $(xy^2)^3$

15. $(x^2y)(3x)$

16. $(x^4y^2)(y^5)$

17. $(-2xy)^3$

18. $(-3x)^2(2y)^3$

19. $(xy^2)^2(5y^3)$

20. $(2y)^4(3y^2)^2$

21. $(-3x)^3(4y^3)^2$

22. $(-xy)^4(xy^8)^2$

23. $(x^2y)(xy^2)^2$

24. $-2x^2y(x^3y^2)^3$

25. **Volume** Find the total volume of four cubic crates identical to the one pictured below.

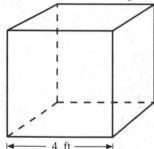

4 ft

26. **Volume** Find the total volume of two cylindrical tanks identical to the one pictured below.

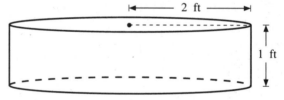

2 ft

1 ft

27. **Savings Account** You put $100 in an account that pays an annual rate of 4%. The balance in the account, A, after t years, is given by $A = 100(1.04)^t$. What is the balance after 2 years?

28. **Collecting Pennies** You collect pennies. You start with one penny and double the number of pennies you have each day for 20 days. How many pennies will you have at the end of 20 days? Is it likely that you will be able to collect this many pennies?

29. **Maps** The scale of a square map indicates that each inch on the map corresponds to 5 miles. Write an expression that describes the area of land shown on the map. If the map is 8 inches on one side, what is the area of land shown on the map?

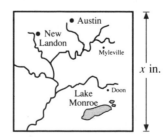

Austin

New Landon

Myleville

x in.

Doon

Lake Monroe

In 1–12, evaluate the expression.

1. 3^{-3}

2. 2^{-5}

3. $\frac{1}{4^{-2}}$

4. $8^0 \cdot 2^{-3}$

5. $3^5 \cdot 3^{-4}$

6. $5^{-7} \cdot 5^9$

7. $9^{-5} \cdot 9^5$

8. $-4 \cdot (-4)^{-3}$

9. $\frac{3^0}{2^{-3}}$

10. $(2^3)^{-2}$

11. $(6^{-1})^2$

12. $(-2^3)^{-1}$

In 13–24, rewrite the expression using positive exponents.

13. x^{-8}

14. $3x^{-5}$

15. $\frac{1}{7x^{-2}}$

16. $\frac{9}{x^{-4}}$

17. $8x^{-7}y^{-8}$

18. $\frac{1}{6x^{-4}y^{-3}z^5}$

19. $\frac{3x^0}{y^{-3}}$

20. $(4x)^{-2}$

21. $(-2x)^{-4}$

22. $\frac{1}{(3x)^{-3}}$

23. $(5x)^0 y^{-2}$

24. $(2x)^{-2} \cdot 3y^5$

25. Sketch the graph of $y = 3^x$.

26. Sketch the graph of $y = \left(\frac{1}{2}\right)^x$.

27. **Radium Isotope** The half-life of the radium isotope Ra^{226} is about 1620 years. If there were initially 100 grams of Ra^{226}, then the number of grams remaining after h half-life periods is $W = 100\left(\frac{1}{2}\right)^h$. Complete the table.

Half-life period, h	0	1	2	3	4	5	6
Grams, W	?	?	?	?	?	?	?

28. **Endangered Species** Between 1980 and 1990 the population of an endangered species decreased at a rate of 0.1% per year. The population, P, in year t is given by $P = 1200(0.999)^t$ where $t = 0$ corresponds to 1985. Find the population of the species in 1980, 1985, 1990, and the projected population in the year 2000.

29. **Nobelium Isotope** The half-life of the Nobelium isotope No^{257} is about 23 seconds. 230 seconds (or 10 half-life periods) after the isotope was released there were 10 grams remaining. The number of grams of No^{257} after h half-life periods is $W = 10\left(\frac{1}{2}\right)^h$ where $h = 0$ corresponds to 230 seconds after the isotope was released. How much No^{257} was initially released?

30. **Town Population** Between 1960 and 1990, the population of a town increased at a rate of 0.34% per year. The population, P, in year t is given by $P = 2000(1.0034)^t$ where $t = 0$ corresponds to 1980. Find the population of the town in 1960, 1970, 1980, and 1990.

In 1–12, evaluate the expression.

1. $\dfrac{7^5}{7^3}$ 2. $\dfrac{6^5}{6^7}$ 3. $\dfrac{18^6}{18^6}$ 4. $\dfrac{(-5)^9}{5^9}$

5. $\dfrac{2^3}{2^{-4}}$ 6. $\dfrac{4^5 \cdot 4^3}{4^6}$ 7. $\dfrac{3^2 \cdot 3^4}{3^9}$ 8. $\left(\dfrac{2}{3}\right)^3$

9. $\left(\dfrac{4}{5}\right)^2$ 10. $\left(-\dfrac{1}{2}\right)^5$ 11. $\left(\dfrac{11}{3}\right)^{-1}$ 12. $\left(\dfrac{3}{2}\right)^{-2}$

In 13–24, simplify the expression.

13. $\left(\dfrac{x}{3}\right)^4$ 14. $\dfrac{x^7}{x^2}$ 15. $\left(\dfrac{2}{x}\right)^6$

16. $x^5 \cdot \dfrac{1}{x^8}$ 17. $x^{12} \cdot \dfrac{1}{x^3}$ 18. $\dfrac{2x^2y}{x^3y^2} \cdot \dfrac{4x^7y^2}{2x^3}$

19. $\dfrac{3xy^4}{2x^5y} \cdot \dfrac{6x^{-3}y^2}{4y}$ 20. $\dfrac{-8x^6y^{-3}}{3x^{-2}y^{-5}} \cdot \dfrac{-6x^{-10}y}{-4x}$ 21. $\dfrac{4x^{-2}y^{-1}}{3x^{-3}} \cdot \dfrac{6x^{-3}y^{-2}}{8y^{-7}}$

22. $\dfrac{(4x^2y^3)^{-1}}{3y} \cdot \dfrac{(2xy^2)^2}{x^{-3}}$ 23. $\left(\dfrac{2x^2y}{3y}\right)^{-3} \cdot \left(\dfrac{4y^3}{x^4}\right)^2$ 24. $\dfrac{5x^{-1}y^3}{xy^{-4}} \cdot \dfrac{(-2x^2)^{-3}}{y}$

25. **Personal Computers** From 1982 to 1992, the cost of manufacturing a PC has decreased by about the same percentage each year. The cost, C (in dollars), in year t can be modeled by $C = 3000(\frac{5}{6})^t$ where $t = 0$ corresponds to 1982. Find the ratio of the cost in 1990 to the cost in 1985.

26. **Assembly Speed** An assembly line worker increases the speed at which he can work by approximately the same percentage for the first 7 months of employment. The speed, s (in parts assembled per hour), in t months can be modeled by $s = 10(1.01)^t$ where $t = 0$ corresponds to the month a worker is hired. Find the ratio of the speed of a worker after 7 months of experience to the speed of a worker after 4 months of experience.

27. **Grade Point Average** From Carmen's freshman year to her senior year, her grade-point average (GPA) increased by approximately the same percentage each year. Carmen's GPA in year t can be modeled by GPA $= 2(\frac{6}{5})^t$ where $t = 0$ corresponds to her freshman year. Complete the table showing Carmen's GPA throughout her high school career.

Year, t	0	1	2	3
GPA	?	?	?	?

28. **Memory** Suppose that you memorized a list of 100 German vocabulary words. Each week you forget $\frac{1}{8}$ of the words you knew the previous week. The number of vocabulary words, V, you remember after t weeks can be modeled by $V = 100(\frac{7}{8})^t$. Complete the table showing the number of words you remember each week.

Week, t	0	5	10	15	20	25	30
Words, V	?	?	?	?	?	?	?

In 1–9, rewrite the scientific notation in decimal form.

1. 2.03×10^3
2. 3.4578×10^4
3. 6.43×10^1

4. 7.2×10^5
5. 5.2×10^0
6. 4.68×10^{-2}

7. 1.3×10^{-6}
8. 8.497×10^{-3}
9. 9.8×10^{-4}

In 10–18, rewrite the decimal in scientific notation.

10. 25,000
11. 36.41
12. 4,000,000

13. 564,200
14. 9.32
15. 0.15

16. 0.0083
17. 0.000000718
18. 0.0673

In 19–27, evaluate the expression without a calculator. Write the answer in scientific notation.

19. $2 \times 10^3 \cdot 3 \times 10^8$
20. $3 \times 10^{-4} \cdot 3 \times 10^{-5}$
21. $2 \times 10^{-5} \cdot 3 \times 10^7$

22. $4 \times 10^{-6} \cdot 2 \times 10^5$
23. $3 \times 10^6 \cdot 4 \times 10^3$
24. $7 \times 10^{-3} \cdot 5 \times 10^{-1}$

25. $3 \times 10^5 \cdot 8 \times 10^{-2}$
26. $12 \times 10^3 \cdot 3 \times 10^{-6}$
27. $6 \times 10^{-8} \cdot 7 \times 10^6$

In 28–33, write the number in scientific notation.

28. **Earth to Pluto** As the planets orbit the sun, the closest Pluto gets to Earth is approximately 2,700,000,000 miles.

29. **Red Blood Cells** The thickness of a red blood cell is approximately 0.0003125 inch.

30. **Human Cells** The body of a human has more than 1,000,000,000,000 cells.

31. **Speed of Light** The speed of light in a vacuum is approximately 186,000 miles per second.

32. **Earth's Diameter** The polar diameter of Earth is approximately 7,900 miles. There are approximately 161,000 cm in one mile. What is the polar diameter of Earth in cm?

33. **Mass of Helium Atom** A proton (P) and a neutron (N) each weigh 1.67×10^{-24} gram. An electron weighs 9.11×10^{-28} gram. Find the mass of one helium atom.

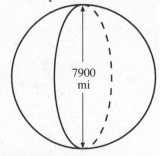

7900 mi

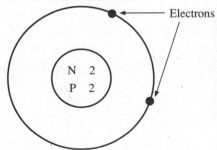

Electrons

N 2
P 2

34. **Surface Area** The total surface area of Earth is about 1.97×10^8 square miles. The surface area of land on Earth is about 5.73×10^7 square miles. Find the ratio of surface area of land to that of the entire planet.

1. **Population Density** In 1990 there were approximately 7×10^6 people living in New York City. New York City has an area of approximately 8.31×10^2 square kilometers. What was the population density (people per square kilometers) of New York City in 1990?

2. **National Debt** The population of the United States is approximately 2.5×10^8. The national debt is approximately $\$1 \times 10^{12}$. How much money would each person have to pay to eliminate the debt?

3. **Typing a Novel** A typist can type 80 words per minute. How long will it take to type an 830-page novel that has an average of 100 words per page?

4. **Ballpark Hotdogs** There are 3×10^4 fans in a stadium watching a game. A hotdog vendor sells $3000 worth of hotdogs at $1.50 each. What was the ratio of hotdogs sold to the number of fans?

5. **Speed of Light** The distance between Saturn and the sun is approximately 8.9×10^8 miles. The speed of light is approximately 1.9×10^5 miles per second. How long does it take light to travel from the sun to Saturn?

6. **Computer Backup** A computer has a hard drive that stores approximately 8.4×10^7 bytes. A high density $5\frac{1}{4}$-inch floppy disk holds approximately 1.3×10^6 bytes. How many floppies are needed to back up the hard drive?

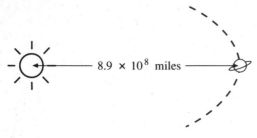

8.9×10^8 miles

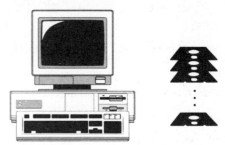

7. **Cost of Land** In 1992, the lot of land shown below cost $\$1.1 \times 10^4$. Find the area (in square feet) of the lot. What was the price of the land per square foot?

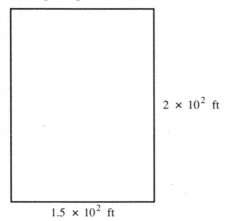

2×10^2 ft

1.5×10^2 ft

8. **Volume of a Virus** A certain virus is shaped like a sphere. The radius of the virus is 9.2×10^{-6} cm. Find the volume of the virus. (Hint: The volume of a sphere is $V = \frac{4}{3}\pi r^3$)

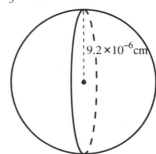

9.2×10^{-6} cm

1. **What is the Balance?** A principal of $200 is deposited in an account that pays 5% interest compounded yearly. Find the balance after 10 years.

2. **What is the Balance?** A principal of $1000 is deposited in an account that pays 6% interest compounded yearly. Find the balance after 3 years.

3. **Money Choices** Which option gives the greater ending balance?
   a. Put $100 in an account that pays 5% interest compounded yearly for 5 years.
   b. Keep $105 in your room and add $4 to it each year for 5 years.

4. **Money Choices** Which option gives the greater ending balance?
   a. Put $100 in an account that pays 8% interest compounded yearly for 10 years.
   b. Put $150 in an account that pays 7% interest compounded yearly for 5 years.

5. **Profit Increases** From 1980 to 1990, the profit earned by a company increased by about 1.5% per year. Use the graph below to write an exponential growth equation.

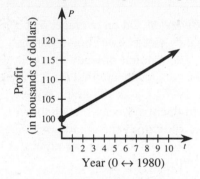

Year (0 ↔ 1980)

6. **College Tuition** From 1980 to 1990, the cost of tuition at a college increased by about 8% per year. Use the graph below to write an exponential growth equation.

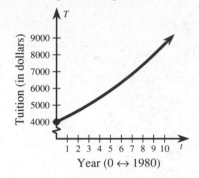

Year (0 ↔ 1980)

In 7 and 8, follow the instructions below.

Write a linear growth equation for the earnings. Write an exponential growth equation showing what the earnings would have been in order to keep up with the inflation rate. From 1975 to 1990, the inflation rate was about 6.2% per year. Let $t = 0$ represent 1975. Did the workers' earnings keep up with inflation?

7. **Manager** From 1975 to 1990, the average weekly salary of a manager increased by $30 per year.

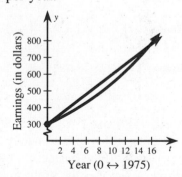

Year (0 ↔ 1975)

8. **Supervisor** From 1975 to 1990, the average weekly salary of a supervisor increased by $35 per year.

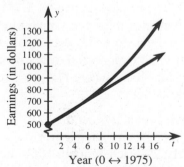

Year (0 ↔ 1975)

1. **Depreciation** In 1990, your family bought a new car for $20,000. Each year the value of the car decreased by 25%. What was the value of the car in 1992? Approximate the value of the car in the year 2000.

2. **Memory** The Sunday before the SAT tests you studied 60 new vocabulary words. The test is on Saturday. How many of the vocabulary words will you remember by Saturday if you forget 3% each day?

3. **Declining Employment** TRL Industries had 14,000 employees in 1980. Each year for 10 years, the number of employees decreased by 4%. Complete the table showing the number of employees for each year. Sketch a graph of the results.

Year	1980	1981	1982	1983	1984	1985	1986	1987	1988	1989	1990
Number of Employees	?	?	?	?	?	?	?	?	?	?	?

4. **Unemployment Rate** In 1987, the unemployment rate of a city decreased by approximately 1.2% each month. In January the unemployment rate was 8%. What was the rate in December?

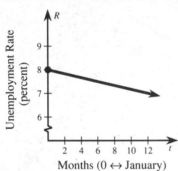

Months (0 ↔ January)

5. **Sleeping Behavior** On an average, as people grow old, they sleep fewer hours during the night. The amount of sleep that your grandfather gets has decreased by 1.5% each year since 1970. Using the graph below write an exponential decay model showing the number of hours your grandfather sleeps per night. How many hours per night did he sleep in 1990?

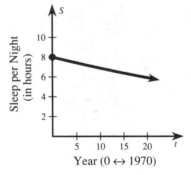

Year (0 ↔ 1970)

6. **Stock** In 1979 your parents bought $300 worth of stock. In 1980 the value of the stock jumped to $600. However, since that time, the stock has decreased in value by 10% per year. Write an exponential decay model to describe the worth of the stock, where $t = 0$ corresponds to 1980. Complete the table.

Year, t	0	1	2	3	4	5	6	7
Value, v	?	?	?	?	?	?	?	?

7. **Population** Between 1960 and 1990 the population of a city decreased by approximately 2% each year. In 1960 the population was 600,000. What was the population in 1990?

8. **Losses** Between 1980 and 1990 the profits of a business decreased by approximately 0.5% each year. In 1980 the business' profit was $1.4 million. What was the profit in 1990?

In 1–12, evaluate the expression. Give the exact value, if possible. Otherwise, give an approximation to two decimal places.

1. $\sqrt{16}$

2. $-\sqrt{64}$

3. $\sqrt{\frac{1}{49}}$

4. $\sqrt{0.25}$

5. $\sqrt{32}$

6. $-\sqrt{36}$

7. $\sqrt{\frac{4}{25}}$

8. $\sqrt{144}$

9. $-\sqrt{108}$

10. $-\sqrt{\frac{36}{121}}$

11. $-\sqrt{1.69}$

12. $\sqrt{\frac{289}{196}}$

In 13–18, evaluate $\sqrt{b^2 - 4ac}$ for the given values of *a*, *b*, and *c*.

13. $a = 1$, $b = 5$, $c = -6$

14. $a = 3$, $b = 6$, $c = 2$

15. $a = 4$, $b = -3$, $c = -1$

16. $a = 3$, $b = -4$, $c = 5$

17. $a = -2$, $b = 7$, $c = -4$

18. $a = 10$, $b = -21$, $c = 9$

In 19–24, use a calculator to evaluate the expression. Round your results to two decimal places. Use estimation to check your results.

19. $\dfrac{6 \pm 2\sqrt{3}}{5}$

20. $\dfrac{3 \pm 5\sqrt{2}}{4}$

21. $\dfrac{-5 \pm 2\sqrt{3}}{3}$

22. $\dfrac{5 \pm 3\sqrt{3}}{2}$

23. $\dfrac{8 \pm 3\sqrt{2}}{-2}$

24. $\dfrac{-2 \pm 3\sqrt{5}}{7}$

25. *Geometry* Use the volume, V, to find the length of the radius. (Use $\pi \approx 3.14$.)

Cylinder: $r = \sqrt{\dfrac{V}{\pi h}}$

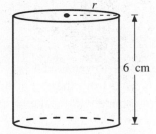

Volume = 230.79 cm

26. *Wheelchair Access* A ramp for a wheelchair access is installed in a building. The height of the ramp is 1 foot. The length of the base of the ramp is 10 feet. How long is the ramp?

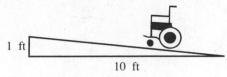

27. *Distance* Sacramento, California is 45 miles north of Stockton, California. Stockton is 48 miles east of Oakland, California. How far is Oakland from Sacramento?

28. *Rescue* A fireman attempts to rescue a person trapped on the second floor of a burning home. The window is 16 feet above the ground. The bottom of the ladder extends 6 feet from the base of the house. How long must the ladder be?

In 1–12, solve the equation.

1. $x^2 = 49$ **2.** $x^2 = 64$ **3.** $3x^2 = 300$ **4.** $8x^2 = 128$

5. $\frac{1}{3}x^2 = 3$ **6.** $\frac{1}{4}x^2 = 9$ **7.** $25x^2 = 4$ **8.** $x^2 + 11 = 12$

9. $x^2 - 56 = 25$ **10.** $3x^2 + 10 = 37$ **11.** $\frac{1}{2}x^2 - 16 = 34$ **12.** $4x^2 - 59 = 62$

In 13–24, use a calculator to solve the equation. Round the results to two decimal places.

13. $x^2 = 35$ **14.** $x^2 = 12$ **15.** $x^2 + 8 = 13$ **16.** $x^2 - 5 = 21$

17. $x^2 + 20 = 37$ **18.** $x^2 - 10 = -3$ **19.** $3x^2 - 31 = 2$ **20.** $\frac{3}{5}x^2 - 8 = 26$

21. $4x^2 + 8 = 19$ **22.** $\frac{1}{2}x^2 + 6 = 9$ **23.** $2x^2 - 22 = 51$ **24.** $\frac{1}{5}x^2 - 11 = 13$

25. *Geometry* The volume of a circular cylinder is 175 square inches. Find the radius. (Use $\pi \approx 3.14$.)

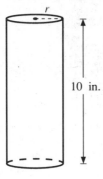

10 in.

$$V = \pi r^2 h$$

26. *Geometry* You live on the end of a cul-de-sac. The area of the cul-de-sac is 1017.36 square feet. What is the radius? (Use $\pi \approx 3.14$.)

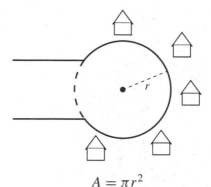

$$A = \pi r^2$$

27. *Dropping a Ball* A ball is dropped from the top of a 300-foot building. How many seconds will it take to hit the ground? $(h = -16t^2 + s)$

28. *Eiffel Tower* The Eiffel Tower is 984 feet tall. If you drop a dime from the top of the tower, how many seconds will it take to hit the ground? $(h = -16t^2 + s)$

Inverse Square Law In 29–30, use the following information.

The intensity, I (in foot-candles), of light falling on a surface is related to the distance, d (in feet), between the light source and the surface by $d^2 = \dfrac{1}{I}$.

29. A flashlight shining onto a wall has an intensity of 0.04 foot-candles. How far is the flashlight from the wall?

30. The electricity goes out and you are reading a book by candlelight. The intensity of the light on the page is 9 foot-candles. How many inches is the flame from the book?

In 1–12, decide whether the graph of the equation opens up or down. Then find the coordinates of the vertex.

1. $y = 3x^2$

2. $y + 2x^2 = 0$

3. $y = 5x^2 - 1$

4. $y = x^2 + 6x$

5. $y - 8 = -3x^2$

6. $y = -2x^2 - 8x$

7. $y = x^2 + 6x + 2$

8. $y = 2x^2 - 4x + 3$

9. $y = 3x^2 - 12x - 2$

10. $y = -2x^2 + 4x - 1$

11. $y - x^2 = 2x + 4$

12. $y + 3 = -x^2 + 4x$

In 13–24, sketch the graph of the equation. Label the vertex.

13. $y = -x^2 - 4$

14. $y = x^2 + 6x + 5$

15. $y = -x^2 - 4x - 3$

16. $y = x^2 + 2x - 15$

17. $y = 2x^2 - x - 1$

18. $y = x^2 - 6x + 10$

19. $y = -2x^2 - 8x + 20$

20. $y = 2x^2 - 6x + 4$

21. $y = -x^2 + 2x + 5$

22. $y = -\frac{1}{3}x^2 + 4x - 7$

23. $y = \frac{1}{2}x^2 + 2x - 1$

24. $y = 2x^2 - \frac{1}{2}x + 1$

25. *Gateway Arch* The Gateway Arch in St. Louis, Missouri, has a shape similar to that of a parabola. The edge of the arch can be modeled by
$$h = -\frac{2}{315}x^2 + \frac{92}{21}x - \frac{880}{7}$$
where x and h are measured in feet. How high is the arch?

26. *Valley Depth* A model for a valley between two mountains whose peaks touch the x-axis is $y = 40.4x^2 - 404x$, where x and y are measured in feet. How deep is the valley?

Throwing a Ball In 27 and 28, use the following information.

The path of a ball thrown into the air from a height of 3 feet is given by $y = -\frac{1}{8}x^2 + x + 3$, where y is the height of the ball in feet at a horizontal distance of x feet from the thrower.

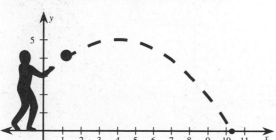

27. How high is the ball at its maximum height?

28. Make a table and estimate the horizontal distance the ball traveled before hitting the ground.

Swish In 29 and 30, use the following information.

In the diagram below, the backboard is located on the y-axis and the hoop is located at the point $(1, 10)$. A basketball thrown toward the hoop follows the path $y = -0.36x^2 + 2.8x + 7.56$ where x and y are measured in feet.

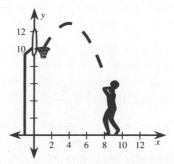

29. When the ball was at its highest point, what was its horizontal distance from the backboard?

30. At its highest point, how far off the ground was the basketball?

In 1–12, use the quadratic formula to solve the equation.

1. $x^2 - 8x + 15 = 0$

2. $x^2 + 11x + 18 = 0$

3. $2x^2 + 3x - 2 = 0$

4. $4x^2 - 7x + 3 = 0$

5. $8x^2 + 26x - 15 = 0$

6. $x^2 + 3x - 5 = 0$

7. $x^2 - 7x + 1 = 0$

8. $3x^2 + 8x + 2 = 0$

9. $3x^2 + x - 6 = 0$

10. $2x^2 - 5x - 8 = 0$

11. $5x^2 - 3x - 5 = 0$

12. $7x^2 - 21x + 8 = 0$

In 13–24, find the x-intercepts of the graph of the equation.

13. $y = x^2 + 2x - 8$

14. $y = 2x^2 - 5x - 3$

15. $y = 6x^2 - x - 12$

16. $y = x^2 + 2x + 8$

17. $y = 3x^2 + 5x + 1$

18. $y = 5x^2 + 50x + 1$

19. $y = 2x^2 - 18x - 3$

20. $y = 4x^2 + 11x - 2$

21. $y = 2x^2 - x + 13$

22. $y = x^2 + 3x + 1$

23. $y = 7x^2 - 12x + 4$

24. $y = 3x^2 + 2x - 34$

25. *Surface Area* The surface area of a rectangular box with a square base is 112 square inches. The surface area is given by $A = 2x^2 + 4xh$. Find x.

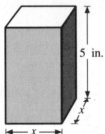

26. *Fireworks* Fireworks are shot upward with an initial velocity of 30 feet per second from a platform 3 feet above the ground. How long will it take the rocket to hit the ground?

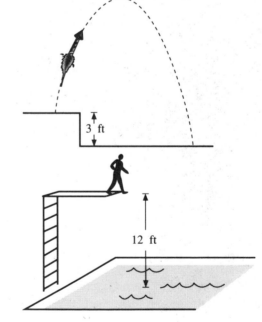

27. *Diving Board* A person steps off a 12-foot high diving board with 0 initial velocity. How many seconds does it take the person to hit the water?

28. *Diving Board* A person springs off a 12-foot high diving board with an initial velocity of 15 feet per second. How many seconds does it take the person to hit the water?

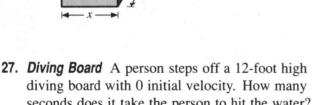

29. *Chemistry Experiment* During a chemistry experiment, the cork in a 0.5-foot tall beaker with an effervescent solution pops off with an initial velocity of 20 feet per second. How many seconds does it take for the cork to hit the table?

In 1–12, decide how many solutions the equation has.

1. $x^2 + 2x + 1 = 0$

2. $2x^2 - 5x - 3 = 0$

3. $x^2 + 4x - 2 = 0$

4. $x^2 + 2x + 6 = 0$

5. $2x^2 + x - 15 = 0$

6. $-3x^2 + 4x + 1 = 0$

7. $2x^2 - x + 16 = 0$

8. $4x^2 + 12x + 9 = 0$

9. $25x^2 - 10x + 1 = 0$

10. $12x^2 - 19x + 5 = 0$

11. $6x^2 + 25x + 21 = 0$

12. $3x^2 - 5x + 4 = 0$

13. **Geometry** Is it possible for the rectangle below to have a perimeter of 32 inches and an area of 70 square inches?

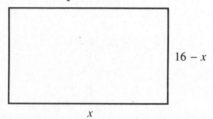

14. **Geometry** Is it possible for the rectangle below to have a perimeter of 40 inches and an area of 75 square inches?

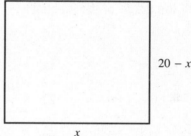

15. **Profit** Your company's profit (in thousands of dollars) for the last 12 years can be modeled by

$$P = \tfrac{10}{3}t^2 + \tfrac{50}{3}t + 100$$

where $t = 0$ corresponds to 1980. If profits continue to rise at this rate, in what year will the company have a profit of $1,100,000?

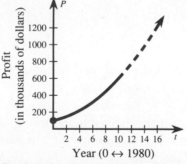

Year (0 ↔ 1980)

16. **Revenue** Between 1980 and 1990, the revenue earned (in thousands of dollars) from exercise equipment can be modeled by

$$R = \tfrac{1}{13}t^2 - \tfrac{11}{65}t + 10$$

where $t = 0$ corresponds to 1980. If the trend continues, in what year will revenue reach $37,000?

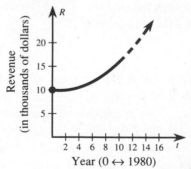

Year (0 ↔ 1980)

Making a Basket In 17 and 18, use the following information.

Patty is only 7 years old, but she insists she can play basketball with a regulation-height hoop. She can throw the ball with an initial velocity of 20 feet per second.

17. Patty needs to be able to throw the ball 7 feet straight up. Can she make a basket?

18. If Patty's dad gets her a 1-foot tall box to stand on, can Patty make a basket?

Name _____

In 1–12, decide whether the point is a solution of the inequality.

1. $y > x^2 + 6x - 3$, $(1, 4)$

2. $y < 3x^2 - 8x - 6$, $(2, -7)$

3. $y \le 3x^2 - 5x - 6$, $(0, -10)$

4. $y > -8x^2 + 4x - 6$, $(-1, -6)$

5. $y > x^2 + 5x - 8$, $(-3, 2)$

6. $y \le -2x^2 - 11x - 4$, $(-4, 9)$

7. $y < 2x^2 - 3x + 4$, $(-1, -8)$

8. $y \ge 2x^2 + 5x + 3$, $(3, 12)$

9. $y \le 4x^2 + 3x + 8$, $(4, 82)$

10. $y \ge 5x^2 - 7x + 2$, $(-3, 28)$

11. $y < 3x^2 + 4x - 15$, $(2, -1)$

12. $y \ge 4x^2 + 10x - 9$, $(-2, 0)$

In 13–24, sketch the graph of the inequality.

13. $y > x^2 - 2x - 8$

14. $y \ge 2x^2 - 5x + 3$

15. $y \ge x^2 + 4x + 2$

16. $y \le -x^2 + 6x + 4$

17. $y < 2x^2 - 5x - 3$

18. $y \ge -3x^2 + 12x - 7$

19. $y \le 12x^2 - 11x - 15$

20. $y > 2x^2 + 3x - 2$

21. $y < -2x^2 + 16x + 1$

22. $y < 2x^2 - 8x + 3$

23. $y \le 2x^2 + 2x + 1$

24. $y > -3x^2 + 2x - 1$

25. **Mounting a Picture** A rectangular picture is twice as long as it is wide and is to be mounted on a mat with the same proportion. Sketch the graph that shows the area of a mat needed to hold a picture of a given length. If the picture is 10 inches wide, can it be mounted on a mat of 110 square inches? Of 210 square inches?

26. **Wrapping** You have a rectangular piece of wrapping paper whose perimeter is at most 20 inches. You want to use it to cover a cubical box of length 2 inches. Sketch the graph that shows the possible area of the paper. Is there a possibility that you could cover the box?

27. **Toy Race Track** A valley on a toy race track can be modeled by $y \le \frac{1}{50}x^2 - \frac{4}{5}x + 10$ where x and y are measured in centimeters. Sketch the graph of the region containing the pillars that support the valley. Find the height of the tallest pillar.

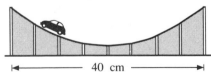

28. **Bridge** The vertical supports on an arch on a bridge can be modeled by $y \le -\frac{1}{500}x^2 + \frac{2}{5}x$ where x and y are measured in meters. Sketch a graph of one arch of the bridge and indicate the possible heights of the supports.

In 1–6, make a scatter plot of the data. Then name the type of model that best fits the data.

1. $(-1, 1)$, $(0, 3)$, $(1, 5)$, $(2, 7)$, $(3, 9)$, $(4, 11)$

2. $(-3, 2)$, $(-2, -1)$, $(-1, -2)$, $(0, -1)$, $(1, 2)$, $(2, 7)$

3. $(-3, 1)$, $(-2, 0)$, $(-1, 1)$, $(0, 2)$, $(1, 3)$, $(2, 4)$

4. $\left(-3, \frac{1}{8}\right)$, $\left(-2, \frac{1}{4}\right)$, $\left(-1, \frac{1}{2}\right)$, $(0, 1)$, $(1, 2)$, $(2, 4)$

5. $(0, 2)$, $(1, 6)$, $(2, 8)$, $(3, 8)$, $(4, 6)$, $(5, 2)$

6. $(-2, 12)$, $(-1, 6)$, $(0, 3)$, $\left(1, \frac{3}{2}\right)$, $\left(2, \frac{3}{4}\right)$, $\left(3, \frac{3}{8}\right)$

7. *Surface Area of a Cube* The surface area, A, of a cube with side, s, is shown in the table. Find a model that relates the surface area and side.

Side, s	1	2	3	4	5	6
Surface Area, A	6	24	54	96	150	216

8. *Simple Interest* The balance, B, in an account that pays 5% interest for t years is shown in the table. Find a model that relates the balance and time.

Time, t	0	1	2	3	4	5
Balance, B	100	105	110	115	120	125

9. *Kinetic Energy* The kinetic (moving) energy, E (in joules), of a 10 kg object moving with velocity, v (in meters per second), is shown in the table. Find a model that relates kinetic energy and velocity.

Velocity, v	0	5	10	15	20
Kenetic Energy, E	0	125	500	1125	2000

10. *Revenue* The table gives the revenue, R (in $1000's), from "how to" books sold at a bookstore between 1980 and 1985. Let t represent the year with $t = 0$ corresponding to 1980. Find a model that relates the revenue and year.

Time, t	0	1	2	3	4	5
Revenue, R	8	10	12.5	15.63	19.53	24.41

11. *Depreciation* The value, V, of a piece of equipment between 1985 and 1990 is given in the table. Let t represent the year with $t = 0$ corresponding to 1985. Find a model that relates the year and value.

Time, t	0	1	2	3	4	5
Value, V ($)	500	450	400	350	300	250

12. *Population* The table gives the population, P (in 10,000's), of a town between 1980 and 1985. Let t represent the year with $t = 0$ corresponding to 1980. Find a model that relates the year and population.

Time, t	0	1	2	3	4	5
Population, P	10	9	8.1	7.29	6.56	5.90

© D. C. Heath and Company

In 1–6, classify the polynomial by degree and by number of terms.

1. 14

2. $2x + 3$

3. $-3x^2 + 6x - 2$

4. $x^3 - 5$

5. $1 - x^4$

6. $x^2 + 4x - x^4 + 3x^3 - 8$

In 7–12, add the polynomials.

7. $3x^2 - 4x + 1; \ -x^2 + x - 9$

8. $6x - 5; \ 4x^3 - 3x + 4$

9. $-8x^2 - 3x + 7; \ -x^3 + 6x^2 - 5$

10. $9x^2 + 3x - 4; \ x^2 - 6x$

11. $4x^3 - 2; \ -x^3 + 3x^2 + x - 1$

12. $x + 3x^3 - 4x^5; \ 2x^3 + 5x^5 - 4$

In 13–18, subtract the second polynomial from the first.

13. $5x + 8; \ 4x^2 - x + 3$

14. $-4x^3 - 8x^2 + 5x + 9; \ 6x^2 + 2x - 4$

15. $-3 + 2x^2 + x^5; \ 4 - x^3 + 2x^2 + x^5$

16. $7x^2 - 3x + 8; \ -3x^2 - 6x + 1$

17. $2x^3 + 4; \ -x^2 + 3x$

18. $6x^3 + 2x^2 - 4x + 1; \ 5x^3 - x^2 + 3x + 4$

In 19–22, perform the indicated operation.

19. $(2x^2 + 3) - (6x + 4) + (3x^2 - x)$

20. $2(x^3 + 3x + 1) - 4(x^2 + 3) - 3(2x^3 + x^2 + 1)$

21. $-3(x^2 + 4) + 2(4x + 1) - 5(3x^2 + 2x - 1)$

22. $5(2x^3 - 3x + 2) - 4(3x^3 + 2x) + 6(4x - 3)$

23. *Photograph Mat* The mat in a frame has an elliptical opening for the photograph. Find the area of the mat. (Area of ellipse: $A = \pi ab$).

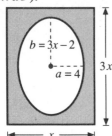

24. *Floor Plan* The first floor of a home has the floor plan shown below. Find the area of the first floor.

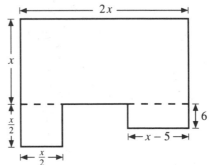

25. *Profit* For 1980 through 1990, the revenue, R, and cost, C, of producing a product can be modeled by

$$R = \tfrac{1}{3}t^2 + \tfrac{20}{3}t + 300$$

$$C = \tfrac{1}{15}t^2 + \tfrac{13}{3}t + 200$$

where $t = 0$ corresponds to 1980. Find a model for the profit earned from 1980 to 1990. (Profit = Revenue − Cost)

26. *Library Books* For 1980 through 1990, the number of fiction books, F (in 10,000's), and nonfiction books, N (in 10,000's), borrowed from a library can be modeled by

$$F = 0.01t^2 + 0.09t + 6$$

$$N = 0.004t^2 + 0.06t + 4$$

where $t = 0$ corresponds to 1980. Find a model for the total number of books borrowed from the library in a year from 1980 to 1990.

In 1–6, multiply.

1. $3x(2x^2 - 5x + 1)$

2. $(4x^2 - 7x)(-x)$

3. $2x^2(x^3 - 2x^2 + 8x - 5)$

4. $(3x^2 - 1)(-6x^3)$

5. $(6x - 5x^2 + 8)(3x)$

6. $-5x^2(2x^3 + 3x^2 - 7x + 9)$

In 7–30, multiply.

7. $(x - 7)(x + 4)$

8. $(x + 5)(x - 6)$

9. $(x - 8)(x - 4)$

10. $(3x + 2)(x + 5)$

11. $(x + 1)(8x - 3)$

12. $(5x - 2)(x - 6)$

13. $(x^2 - 3)(x + 4)$

14. $(x + 5)(x^2 + 4x)$

15. $(\frac{1}{2}x + 3)(4x + 5)$

16. $(\frac{1}{3}x - 2)(\frac{1}{2}x + 6)$

17. $(x - \frac{1}{2})(2x - \frac{1}{3})$

18. $(3x + 2)(2x + 5)$

19. $(2x - 1)(6x - 7)$

20. $(5x + 2)(8x - 3)$

21. $(4x - 9)(3x + 1)$

22. $(2x^2 + 4)(3x + 1)$

23. $(6x + 5)(5x^2 - 2)$

24. $(4x - 1)(8x^2 + 3)$

25. $(4x^2 + 3x)(5x - 3)$

26. $(2x^2 - 6x)(7x + 1)$

27. $(3x^2 - 4x - 7)(x + 5)$

28. $(2x^2 + 3x + 5)(x^2 - 3)$

29. $(2x - 3)(x^2 + 3x - 1)$

30. $(4x^2 - 6x + 4)(3x + 2)$

31. **Floor Plan** The floor plan of a home is shown below. Find an expression for the area of the home. What is the area if $x = 20$ ft?

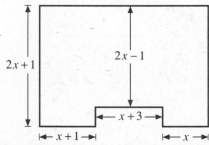

32. **Volume** Find an expression for the volume of the box. What is the volume if $x = 2$ in.?

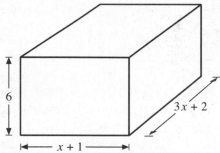

33. **Exercise Bike** You ride an exercise bike that has an electronic odometer and clock. Each week you increase the rate, R, and time, T, at which you ride the bike. The equation $R = \frac{2}{5}x + 14$ models the rate at which you ride where R is measured in mph and $x = 0$ corresponds to week 0. The equation $T = \frac{1}{30}x + \frac{1}{12}$ models the amount of time you ride at each workout, where T is measured in hours and $x = 0$ corresponds to week 0. Find a model for the distance you ride in a workout.

34. **Walking Shoe Inventory** For 1980 through 1990, the number of walking shoes in stock at a shoe store can be modeled by $S = 2.5t^2 + 5t + 100$ where S is the number of pairs and $t = 0$ corresponds to 1980. The cost per pair to the shoe store, C, can be modeled by $C = 0.1t + 30$ where C is measured in dollars and $t = 0$ corresponds to 1980. Find a model for the total cost of walking shoes per year for the store.

In 1–12, write the square as a trinomial.

1. $(x + 5)^2$

2. $(x - 6)^2$

3. $(x + 9)^2$

4. $(2x + 1)^2$

5. $(4x - 1)^2$

6. $(x + 7)^2$

7. $(x - 2)^2$

8. $(3x - 4)^2$

9. $(3x + 8)^2$

10. $(x - 3)^2$

11. $(5x - 2)^2$

12. $(4x + 5)^2$

In 13–24, multiply.

13. $(x + 3)(x - 3)$

14. $(x - 7)(x + 7)$

15. $(2x + 1)(2x - 1)$

16. $(4x - 3)(4x + 3)$

17. $(3x + 3)(3x - 3)$

18. $(5x + 2)(5x - 2)$

19. $(2x - 3)(2x + 3)$

20. $(7x - 5)(7x + 5)$

21. $(x + y)(x - y)$

22. $(5x - y)(5x + y)$

23. $(x + 4y)(x - 4y)$

24. $(2x + 3y)(2x - 3y)$

25. **Area Model** Find an expression for the area of the shaded region shown below. Then evaluate the expression when x is equal to 5 inches; to 6 inches; and to 7 inches.

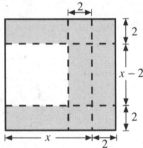

26. **Area Model** Find an expression for the area of the shaded region shown below. Then evaluate the expression when x is equal to 5 inches; to 7 inches; and to 9 inches.

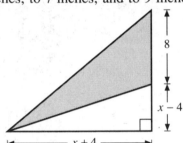

27. **Total Profit** For 1980 through 1990, the number of units, N, produced by a manufacturing plant can be modeled by $N = 2t + 3$ where N is measured in thousands of units and $t = 0$ corresponds to 1980. The profit per unit, P, can be modeled by $P = 2t - 3$ where P is measured in dollars and $t = 0$ corresponds to 1980. Find an expression for the total profit, T, where T is measured in thousands of dollars. What was the total profit in 1985?

28. **Blue Eyes-Brown Eyes** In humans, the brown eye gene, B, is dominant and the blue eye gene b, is recessive. This means that humans whose eye genes are BB, Bb, or bB have brown eyes and those with bb have blue eyes. The Punnett square at the right shows the results of eye colors for children of parents who each have one B gene and one b gene. What percentage of children will have brown eyes? What percentage will have blue eyes? Use the model $(0.5B + 0.5b)^2 = 0.25BB + 0.5Bb + 0.25bb$ to answer the question.

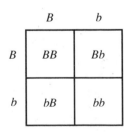

In 1–12, factor out the greatest common monomial factor.

1. $3x^2 + 18$

2. $6x - 12$

3. $5x^2 - 25$

4. $4x + 10$

5. $8x^2 + 4$

6. $2x^2 + 8x$

7. $7x^2 - 21x$

8. $6x^2 - 9x$

9. $10x^2 + 35x$

10. $20x^2 + 6x$

11. $2x^2 + 4x - 8$

12. $12x^2 - 9x + 15$

In 13–27, factor the expression.

13. $x^2 - 49$

14. $x^2 + 12x + 36$

15. $4x^2 + 12x + 9$

16. $8x^2 - 8x + 2$

17. $9x^2 - 121$

18. $9x^2 + 6x + 1$

19. $x^2 - 16x + 64$

20. $12x^2 - 75$

21. $\frac{1}{9}x^2 - \frac{1}{4}$

22. $25x^2 - 20x + 4$

23. $5x^2 + 20x + 20$

24. $49x^2 - 14x + 1$

25. $9x^2 - 30x + 25$

26. $49 - (x + 2)^2$

27. $20 - 5(x - 3)^2$

In 28–30, use the technique described in Example 4 to find the indicated right triangle triple. (Exercise 28 has 2 solutions.)

28. $9^2 + b^2 = c^2$

29. $10^2 + b^2 = c^2$

30. $11^2 + b^2 = c^2$

31. *Trapezoid* The formula for the area of a trapezoid is $A = \frac{1}{2}h(b_1 + b_2)$. Derive this formula by finding the sum of the areas of the rectangle and triangle that make up the trapezoid.

32. *Washers* Washers are available in various sizes. Find an expression for the area of one flat side of a washer. Factor the expression. What is the area if $x = 5$ cm and $y = 2$ cm?

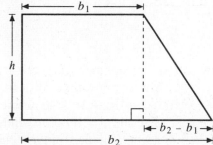

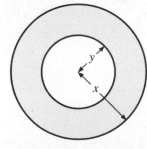

33. *Quilt* A square quilt for a child's bed has a border made up of 36 pieces with an area of x each, and 4 small squares with an area of 1 square inch each. The main part of the quilt is made up of 81 squares with an area of x^2 each. Find an expression for the area of the quilt. Factor the expression. If the quilt is 5 ft by 5 ft, what are the dimensions of the inside squares?

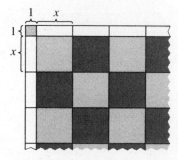

In 1–12, factor the trinomial.

1. $x^2 + 8x + 15$

2. $x^2 - 5x + 4$

3. $x^2 - x - 42$

4. $x^2 + 6x - 16$

5. $2x^2 - 5x - 3$

6. $3x^2 + 10x - 8$

7. $7x^2 - 31x + 12$

8. $5x^2 + 7x + 2$

9. $6x^2 - 11x + 3$

10. $30x^2 + x - 1$

11. $20x^2 - 7x - 6$

12. $10x^2 + 17x + 3$

In 13–24, use the discriminant to decide whether the polynomial can be factored with integer coefficients. If it can, factor it.

13. $8x^2 + 2x - 3$

14. $x^2 + 2x + 2$

15. $x^2 - 7x + 7$

16. $4x^2 + 8x - 12$

17. $3x^2 + 2x - 2$

18. $12x^2 + 16x - 3$

19. $4x^2 - 3x + 8$

20. $2x^2 - 5x - 6$

21. $2 - 13x + 15x^2$

22. $6 - 5x - 4x^2$

23. $3x^2 + 8x + 3$

24. $2x^2 - 6x + 3$

25. **Geometry** The area of a parallelogram is given by $A = x^2 + 4x - 12$. Find expressions for possible lengths and heights of the parallelogram.

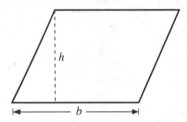

26. **Geometry** The area of a triangle is given by $A = x^2 + \frac{11}{2}x + \frac{5}{2}$. Find an expression for possible bases and heights of the triangle. (Hint: First factor out $\frac{1}{2}$.)

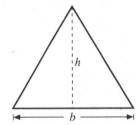

27. **Summer Reading** The library sponsored a summer reading program for children. The number of children participating, C, each week can be modeled by $C = t^2 + 10t + 16$ where t represents the week and $t = 0$ corresponds to the first week. The first week there are 2 groups of children. Each week, for 5 weeks, a new group is added. Find a model for the average number of children in each group. Use the model to find the number of children in each group during each week.

28. **Summer Job** Every summer you work at a grocery store. Your daily wages, W, can be modeled by $W = -\frac{1}{4}t^2 - 3t + 40$ where t represents the year and $t = 0$ corresponds to the summer of 1988. The first summer you work 8 hours a day. Each summer for the next 4 years you work 1 hour less per day. Find a model for your average hourly wage each summer. Use the model to find your hourly rate during each summer.

In 1–12, solve the equation by factoring.

1. $x^2 + x - 6 = 0$

2. $x^2 - 8x + 15 = 0$

3. $3x^2 + 9x - 12 = 0$

4. $6x^2 - 10x - 4 = 0$

5. $6x^2 - 27x + 27 = 0$

6. $3x^2 + 5x + 2 = 0$

7. $8x^2 + 10x + 3 = 0$

8. $4x^2 - 8x - 5 = 0$

9. $12x^2 - 5x - 3 = 0$

10. $15x^2 + 16x - 15 = 0$

11. $8x^2 - 22x + 5 = 0$

12. $6x^2 + 5x + 1 = 0$

In 13–24, solve the equation by finding square roots, by the quadratic formula, or by factoring.

13. $4x^2 - 9 = 0$

14. $x^2 + 6x = 0$

15. $x^2 - 4x + 1 = 0$

16. $x^2 + 21 = 10x$

17. $x^2 + 7x = 1$

18. $2x^2 - 3x - 4 = 0$

19. $2x^2 = 16x$

20. $2x^2 + 12x + 10 = -8$

21. $2x^2 - x = 6$

22. $12x^2 + x - 1 = 0$

23. $2x^2 + 7x = 4$

24. $2x^2 + 3x + 5 = 8$

In 25–27, find the dimensions of the geometric shape.

25.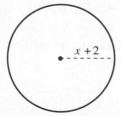

Area $= 144\,\pi\,\text{cm}^2$

26.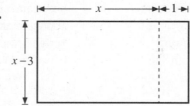

Area $= 60$ in.^{2}

27.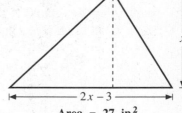

Area $= 27$ in.^{2}

28. **Throwing a Ball** A ball is thrown into the air with an initial velocity of 13 feet per second. The ball was 3 feet off the ground when it was released. The equation $h = -16t^2 + 13t + 3$ models the height of the ball. How long does it take for the ball to hit the ground $(h = 0)$?

29. **Making a Box** You construct a box with a volume of 110 cubic inches from a piece of metal by cutting 2-inch squares from each corner and folding up the sides. Find the dimensions of the box. Find the dimensions of the original piece of metal.

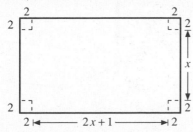

30. **Fencing** You are buying a fence to enclose a garden that has an area of 170 square feet. What are the dimensions of the area to be enclosed? How much fencing do you need?

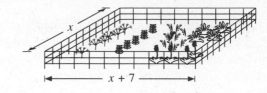

© D. C. Heath and Company

In 1–12, solve the equation by completing the square.

1. $x^2 + 10x - 4 = 0$ 2. $x^2 + 6x - 1 = 0$ 3. $x^2 - 8x + 3 = 0$

4. $x^2 - 6x - 8 = 0$ 5. $x^2 + 12x - 3 = 0$ 6. $x^2 + 4x + 2 = 0$

7. $x^2 - 10x + 4 = 0$ 8. $x^2 + 8x + 8 = 0$ 9. $2x^2 + 8x - 6 = 0$

10. $2x^2 - 16x + 4 = 0$ 11. $3x^2 + 12x - 6 = 0$ 12. $5x^2 - 10x - 20 = 0$

In 13–24, use the most convenient method to solve the equation.

13. $x^2 - 7x + 12 = 0$ 14. $9x^2 - 27x = 0$ 15. $3x^2 - 15 = 0$

16. $x^2 + 4x - 4 = 0$ 17. $9x^2 + 2 = 27$ 18. $2x^2 + x - 3 = 0$

19. $2x^2 + 8x + 3 = 10$ 20. $3x^2 + 4x - 2 = 0$ 21. $5x^2 - x - 2 = 0$

22. $6x^2 + 11x = -3$ 23. $x^2 - 20x + 60 = 0$ 24. $x^2 + 5 = 7x$

25. **Population Growth** In 1990, the populations of two neighboring towns were 20,000. From 1990 to 1992, the population of one town grew exponentially. In 1992, its population was 24,200. The population of the second town also grew exponentially, but at a rate 2% slower per year than the first town. What was the population of the second town in 1992?

26. **Distance** Worth, Missouri is 25 miles more north of Independence, Missouri than it is west of Putnam, Missouri. The distance between Independence and Putnam is approximately 120 miles. Find the distance between Putnam and Worth and the distance between Worth and Independence.

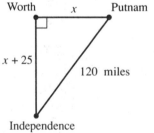

27. **Diver** The path followed by a diver can be modeled by $h = -\frac{1}{6}(x^2 - 5x - 66)$ where h is the height (in feet) and x is the horizontal distance (in feet) from the edge of the pool. How far from the edge of the pool is the diver when he hits the water?

28. **Tunnel Length** A tunnel goes through a mountain whose shape can be modeled by $h = -64x^2 + 16x$ where h is the height (in miles) and x is the distance (in miles) from the opening of the tunnel. Find the length of the tunnel.

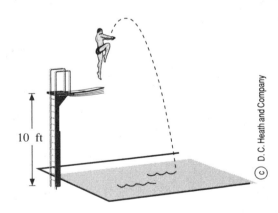

In 1–18, solve the proportion.

1. $\dfrac{x}{3} = \dfrac{4}{5}$

2. $-\dfrac{x}{5} = \dfrac{1}{2}$

3. $\dfrac{8}{x} = \dfrac{12}{7}$

4. $\dfrac{5}{11} = \dfrac{3}{x}$

5. $-\dfrac{6}{7} = \dfrac{3}{x}$

6. $\dfrac{2x}{3} = \dfrac{1}{7}$

7. $-\dfrac{5x}{2} = \dfrac{9}{4}$

8. $\dfrac{x+1}{3} = \dfrac{1}{2}$

9. $\dfrac{2}{x-3} = \dfrac{5}{x+1}$

10. $\dfrac{x}{5} = \dfrac{1}{x+4}$

11. $\dfrac{5x}{x+7} = \dfrac{x}{x-1}$

12. $\dfrac{x}{2} = \dfrac{3x+8}{x}$

13. $\dfrac{14}{x+4} = \dfrac{x+1}{x-1}$

14. $\dfrac{x+5}{x+1} = \dfrac{5}{x-2}$

15. $\dfrac{x+2}{-x} = \dfrac{2}{x+3}$

16. $\dfrac{x-4}{x-2} = \dfrac{1}{x-4}$

17. $\dfrac{x+3}{x} = \dfrac{x-3}{2}$

18. $\dfrac{x}{2x-6} = \dfrac{x+4}{15}$

19. **Ship Model** You are making a model of the QE II. The ratio of the model to actual size is 1 to 500. The model is approximately 23.1 inches long. Estimate the actual length of the QE II.

20. **Statue of Liberty** There is a model of the Statue of Liberty on a small island in the Seine River in France. The ratio of the model to actual size is 1 to 4. From her feet to the tip of the torch, the actual statue measures 1813 inches. Estimate the height of the model.

Statue of Liberty In 21 and 22, use the following information.

The Statue of Liberty is approximately 27 times life size.

21. Estimate the length of the nose. (Assume that the average length of a woman's nose is 2 inches.)

22. Estimate the distance across each eye. (Assume that the average woman's eye is 1.1 inch across.)

23. **Architectural Firm** An architectural firm makes a model of a science center they are building. The ratio of the model to actual size is 1 to 80. Estimate the height of the model if the actual building is 60 feet high.

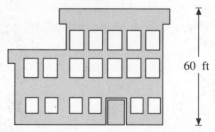

60 ft

24. **Hoagie Sale** Your class sold hoagies to raise money for the prom. The homerooms which sold the most were Mr. Saunders' and Mrs. Lorigan's homerooms. The ratio of the number of students in Mr. Saunders' homeroom to Mrs. Lorigan's homeroom was about the same as the ratio of money earned in each homeroom, respectively. Mr. Saunders has 30 students in his homeroom and they sold $100 worth of hoagies. Mrs. Lorigan's homeroom sold $90 worth of hoagies. How many students are in her homeroom?

In 1–12, solve the percent problem.

1. What number is 15% of 60?

2. 24 is what percent of 200?

3. 66 is 11% of what number?

4. What number is 32% of 500?

5. 6 is 5% of what number?

6. 16 is what percent of 25?

7. 308 is what percent of 350?

8. 36 is 45% of what number?

9. What number is 73% of 300?

10. What number is 66% of 210?

11. 110 is what percent of 250?

12. 42 is 60% of what number?

Geometry **In 13 and 14, what percent of the region is shaded?**

13.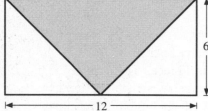

14.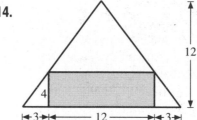

15. *Earth's Surface Area* Earth is approximately 30% land. There are approximately 57,280,000 square miles of land on Earth. What is the total surface area of Earth?

16. *Population of the United States* In 1990, California was the state with the largest population, 2.984×10^7. This was approximately 12% of the total population of the United States. Estimate the population of the United States in 1990.

Transportation **In 17–20, use the following information.**

In 1989, the means of transportation to work were as follows.

85.7%	Private automobile
5.9%	Public transportation
1.3%	Bicycle or motorcycle
3.9%	Foot
2.3%	Work at home
0.9%	Other

Your school has 110 employees.

17. Estimate how many drive private cars to work.

18. Estimate how many take public transportation.

19. Estimate how many ride a bicycle or motorcycle to work.

20. Estimate how many walk to work.

In 21–24, use the following information.

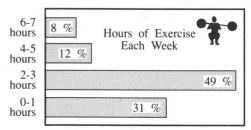

Two hundred people were asked how many hours a week they exercise.

21. How many people exercised 6–7 hr per week?

22. How many people exercised 4–5 hr per week?

23. How many people exercised 2–3 hr per week?

24. How many people exercised 0–1 hr per week?

© D. C. Heath and Company

In 1–6, the variables x and y vary directly. Given one pair of values for x
and y, find an equation that relates the variables.

1. $x = 4$, $y = 32$ **2.** $x = 36$, $y = 9$ **3.** $x = 15$, $y = 35$

4. $x = 16$, $y = 10$ **5.** $x = 24$, $y = 9$ **6.** $x = 8$, $y = 12$

In 7–12, the variables x and y vary inversely. Given one pair of values for x
and y, find an equation that relates the variables.

7. $x = 3$, $y = 7$ **8.** $x = 5$, $y = 2$ **9.** $x = 4$, $y = 6$

10. $x = 1$, $y = 8$ **11.** $x = \frac{1}{2}$, $y = 10$ **12.** $x = \frac{2}{3}$, $y = 5$

In 13–18, assume the variables vary directly.

13. If $x = 2$ when $y = 8$, find x when $y = 16$.   **14.** If $x = 14$ when $y = 7$, find x when $y = 5$.

15. If $x = 3$ when $y = 4$, find x when $y = 24$.   **16.** If $x = 6$ when $y = 10$, find x when $y = 2$.

17. If $x = 18$ when $y = 4$, find x when $y = 1$.   **18.** If $x = 30$ when $y = 8$, find x when $y = 4$.

In 19–24, assume the variables vary inversely.

19. If $x = 6$ when $y = 2$, find x when $y = 4$.   **20.** If $x = 2$ when $y = 7$, find x when $y = 8$.

21. If $x = 3$ when $y = 5$, find x when $y = 20$.   **22.** If $x = \frac{1}{3}$ when $y = 18$, find x when $y = 3$.

23. If $x = \frac{2}{3}$ when $y = 4$, find x when $y = 2$.   **24.** If $x = \frac{1}{4}$ when $y = \frac{5}{3}$, find x when $y = 10$.

In 25 and 26, find an equation that relates the two variables.

25. *Circumference and Radius* The circumference
of a circle varies directly with the length of
the radius. When the circumference is
8π in., the radius is 4 in.

26. *Radio Waves* The frequency, f, in hertz
(vibrations per second) of a radio wave
varies inversely with the wavelength, γ,
in meters per vibration. When the frequency
is 1.024×10^5 hertz the wavelength is 2.92
meters.

27. *Ohm's Law* The electromotive force, E (in volts),
varies directly with the current, I (in amperes),
flowing through a given conductor. A current
of 4 amperes passing through the conductor has
an electromotive force of 8 volts. What is the
electromotive force if 3 amperes pass through the
conductor?

28. *Hooke's Law* The force required to stretch a spring,
F, varies directly with the amount the spring is
stretched, s. Ten pounds is needed to stretch a
spring 10 inches. How much force is required to
stretch the spring 4 inches?

1. **Throwing a Die** What is the probability that you will roll a 5 on a toss of a die?

2. **Raffle Tickets** You buy 5 raffle tickets. What is the probability that you will win if 200 tickets were sold?

3. **Gymnastics** During a difficult release move, a gymnast has fallen from the parallel bars in 2 of the 12 competitions this season. The state meet is next week. What is the probability that she will successfully complete the release move?

4. **4th Down Conversions** During a game, the Pittsburgh Steelers converted 6 of 11 fourth downs into first downs. With only minutes left in the game, it is fourth down again and they must make a first down to continue their drive. What is the probability that they will make the first down?

5. **Defects** A machine shop averages 2 defects per million parts made. If you randomly select a part from a box, what is the probability that the part is defective?

6. **Population of Iowa** The population of the United States is about 2.5×10^8. The probability that a citizen lives in Iowa is 0.011. What is the population of Iowa?

7. **Degrees** In 1989, 1,266,282 people earned bachelor's, master's, or doctoral degrees. The probability that a master's degree is earned is 0.235. How many master's degrees were earned?

8. **Carnival Game** You throw a beanbag at a wall with 7 colored squares, each with an area of $\frac{1}{4}$ ft^2. If you hit a square, you win a prize. The area of the wall is 40 ft^2. What is the probability that you win a prize?

Favorite Subjects In 9–12, use the following information.

Senior class members were asked to name their favorite subject. The results of the survey of the 220 students are listed in the table below.

Subject	English	Social Studies	Science	Math	Foreign Language	Gym	No Preference
Number	30	40	50	35	20	10	35

9. What is the probability that a student said math?

10. What is the probability that a student said English?

11. What is the probability that a student said social studies?

12. What is the probability that a student said science?

13. The table shows the areas of the seven continents on Earth. The total area of Earth is about 1.97×10^8 square miles. What is the probability that a meteorite will fall on each of the continents?

Continent	Area (square miles)
Asia	16,966,000
Africa	11,706,000
North America	9,417,000
South America	6,884,000
Antarctica	5,100,000
Europe	4,063,000
Australia	2,968,000

In 1–12, find the domain of the rational expression.

1. $\dfrac{3}{x-2}$ **2.** $\dfrac{-4}{x+3}$ **3.** $\dfrac{x}{x^2-x}$ **4.** $\dfrac{x+6}{x+4}$

5. $\dfrac{8}{x^2-4}$ **6.** $\dfrac{x+3}{x^2-16}$ **7.** $\dfrac{x-7}{x^2-49}$ **8.** $\dfrac{x^2-2x-3}{x^2-9}$

9. $\dfrac{5}{x^2+3x+2}$ **10.** $\dfrac{x+3}{x^2-x-12}$ **11.** $\dfrac{x-4}{2x^2+x-1}$ **12.** $\dfrac{x^2-4x}{3x^2-14x+8}$

In 13–24, simplify the expression.

13. $\dfrac{7x}{21}$ **14.** $\dfrac{20x}{28}$ **15.** $\dfrac{18x^2}{12x}$

16. $\dfrac{36x^4}{42x^7}$ **17.** $\dfrac{5x}{x^2+3x}$ **18.** $\dfrac{2x^2+x}{4x}$

19. $\dfrac{x^2-1}{6x+6}$ **20.** $\dfrac{4x-12}{x^2-9}$ **21.** $\dfrac{x^2-3x-10}{x^2+5x+6}$

22. $\dfrac{2x^2+5x+3}{4x^2+4x-3}$ **23.** $\dfrac{x^2+10x+24}{x^2-16}$ **24.** $\dfrac{x^3-x^2-12x}{x^3-9x}$

Advertisement Flyers In 25 and 26, use the following information.

The number of advertisement flyers, A (in 100,000's), sent out by a department store between 1980 and 1990 can be modeled by

$$A = \dfrac{6t^2+102t+312}{(18-0.5t+0.01t^2)(t+13)}$$

where $t = 0$ corresponds to 1980.

25. Simplify the expression for A.

26. How many flyers were mailed in 1990?

Material Used In 27 and 28, use the following information.

The material consumed (in 1000's of pounds) by a plastic injection molding machine per year between 1980 and 1990 can be modeled by

$$M = \dfrac{8t^2+67t+77}{(3-0.2t+0.1t^2)(t+7)}$$

where $t = 0$ corresponds to 1980.

27. Simplify the expression for M.

28. How much material was consumed in 1990?

29. *Tapestry* Find an expression for the area of a tapestry hanging on a museum wall. Find an expression for the area of the wall. Find an expression for the ratio of the area of the tapestry to the area of the wall and simplify the expression.

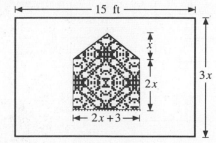

30. *Room Addition* Blueprints of 2 square rooms are redrawn to increase the length of both rooms by 6 feet and decrease the width of the rooms by 3 feet and 2 feet, respectively. Find an expression for the ratio of the area of the revised room 1 to the area of the revised room 2.

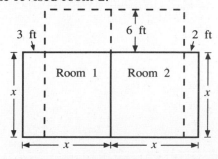

In 1–24, simplify the expression.

1. $\dfrac{4x}{3} \cdot \dfrac{2}{x}$

2. $\dfrac{7x}{5} \cdot \dfrac{10}{x^2}$

3. $\dfrac{12x^3}{25} \cdot \dfrac{40}{9x^2}$

4. $\dfrac{14x^5}{3x^2} \cdot \dfrac{9x^3}{28x^8}$

5. $\dfrac{6 - 18x}{4x^2} \cdot \dfrac{x^3}{2 - 6x}$

6. $\dfrac{6}{x^2 - 9x + 20} \cdot (5x - 25)$

7. $\dfrac{4x}{x + 1} \cdot \dfrac{x^2 - 6x - 7}{x^3 + 7x^2}$

8. $\dfrac{x}{2x^2 - 7x + 3} \cdot (7x - 21)$

9. $\dfrac{2x - 6}{x^2 - 25} \cdot \dfrac{x^2 + 6x + 5}{x^2 - 9}$

10. $\dfrac{16x}{25x^2 - 9} \cdot \dfrac{25x^2 + 30x + 9}{8x}$

11. $\dfrac{1}{x^2 + 5x - 24} \cdot \dfrac{x^2 + 6x - 16}{3x}$

12. $\dfrac{x^2 + x - 6}{x^2 - x - 2} \cdot \dfrac{x^2 + 5x + 4}{x^2 + 2x - 3}$

13. $\dfrac{4x^2}{9} \div \dfrac{8x^3}{3x^5}$

14. $\dfrac{x + 3}{-4} \div \dfrac{x + 3}{5}$

15. $\dfrac{3x}{x - 2} \div \dfrac{4x^5}{x - 2}$

16. $\dfrac{x - 7}{x^2 - 1} \div \dfrac{x - 7}{x^2 + x}$

17. $\dfrac{3x}{-7x + 7} \div \dfrac{9x}{3x - 3}$

18. $\dfrac{x + 3}{x^2 - 3x - 10} \div \dfrac{x + 3}{8x + 16}$

19. $\dfrac{x^2 - 4x + 4}{x + 8} \div (x - 2)$

20. $\dfrac{x^2 + 7x + 10}{x^2 - 2x - 35} \div (8x + 16)$

21. $\dfrac{x^2 - 5x + 4}{x^2 + 3x} \div \dfrac{x^2 - 3x - 4}{2x^2 + 6x}$

22. $\dfrac{x^2 - 36}{2x^2 + 3x + 1} \div \dfrac{4x - 24}{8x + 4}$

23. $\left(\dfrac{3x^2}{8x^5} \cdot 2x^3 \right) \div \dfrac{9x}{8x^2}$

24. $\left(\dfrac{x}{x + 2} \cdot \dfrac{4}{x^3} \right) \div \dfrac{2x - 2}{x + 2}$

25. **Total Cost** The cost of producing a product, C (in dollars), from 1980 to 1990 can be modeled by
$$C = \dfrac{10 + 3t}{100 - t}$$
where $t = 0$ corresponds to 1980. The number of units made each year (in hundreds of thousands of units) between 1980 and 1990 can be modeled by
$$N = \dfrac{200 - 2t}{11 - t}$$
where $t = 0$ corresponds to 1980. Find an expression that models the total production costs per year. Simplify the expression.

26. **Profit per Unit** The total profit earned (in millions of dollars) from 1980 to 1990 by a manufacturer can be modeled by
$$P = \dfrac{3500 + 500t}{105 - t}$$
where $t = 0$ corresponds to 1980. The number of units sold (in hundreds of thousands of units) from 1980 to 1990 can be modeled by
$$N = \dfrac{(7 + t)(3000 - 20t)}{630 - 6t}$$
where $t = 0$ corresponds to 1980. Find an expression that models the profit per unit earned each year. Simplify the expression.

27. **Geometry** Find an expression that describes the number of 2-inch by 3-inch tiles that can be placed in the rectangle.

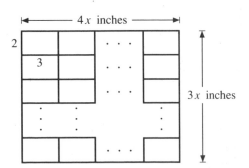

© D. C. Heath and Company

In 1–12, divide.

1. $(24x - 16) \div 4$

2. $(3x^2 + 8x - 2) \div 2$

3. $(x^2 + 4) \div 3$

4. $(7x^2 + 5x - 2) \div x$

5. $(x^3 + x + 5) \div x$

6. $(x^{10} - 18) \div x$

7. $(9x^3 + 3x^2 - 6x + 1) \div (-x)$

8. $(3x^2 + 18x) \div 3x$

9. $(-8x^3 + 4x^2 - 5x - 6) \div (-x)$

10. $(6x^2 - 4x + 5) \div 2x$

11. $(10x^3 + 8x^2 - 7x - 1) \div 2x$

12. $(16x^3 + 8x^2 - 4x + 2) \div 4x$

In 13–24, divide. Write the result as Quotient + $\dfrac{\text{Remainder}}{\text{Divisor}}$.

13. $(2x - 1) \div (x + 3)$

14. $(13x + 4) \div (x - 2)$

15. $(2x^2 - 6x + 3) \div (x - 1)$

16. $(x^2 - 8) \div (x - 2)$

17. $(5x^2 + 16x) \div (x + 3)$

18. $(3x^2 - 10x - 15) \div (x - 5)$

19. $(x^2 + 4x - 6) \div (x - 4)$

20. $(9x - 8) \div (3x - 1)$

21. $(10x + 28) \div (2x + 5)$

22. $(10x^2 + 4x + 7) \div (2x + 1)$

23. $(4x^2 - 8x + 2) \div (2x - 3)$

24. $(24x^2 - 6x - 5) \div (4x + 1)$

25. *Geometry* If the rectangle below is divided into 4 equal pieces, find the area of each piece.

$4x + 6$

26. *Geometry* If the rectangle below is divided into x equal pieces, find the area of each piece.

$4x - 3$

27. *Car Dealer* The number of sports cars that a dealer sells per year between 1980 and 1990 can be modeled by $S = 5t + 23$ where $t = 0$ corresponds to 1980. The total number of cars sold by the dealer can be modeled by $C = 20t + 168$. Use long division to find a model for the ratio of sports cars sold to the total number of cars sold. Use the model to complete the table. Are sports cars becoming more or less important to the dealer's business?

Year, t	0	2	4	6	8	10
Ratio of S to C	?	?	?	?	?	?

28. *Ice Cream vs Yogurt* From 1980 to 1990, the number of desserts sold at an ice cream and yogurt stand can be modeled by $D = 4(t + 5)$ (in thousands of desserts), where $t = 0$ corresponds to 1980. The number of ice cream desserts sold can be modeled by $I = 2(t + 15)$ (in thousands of desserts). Use long division to find a model for the ratio of ice cream desserts sold and total desserts sold. Use the model to complete the table. Is ice cream becoming more or less popular than frozen yogurt?

Year, t	0	2	4	6	8	10
Ratio of I to D	?	?	?	?	?	?

© D. C. Heath and Company

11.8

Name _____

In 1–12, solve the equation by cross multiplying.

1. $\dfrac{x}{2} = \dfrac{6}{7}$

2. $\dfrac{4}{3} = \dfrac{8}{x}$

3. $\dfrac{2}{x} = \dfrac{5}{2x + 3}$

4. $\dfrac{x}{5} = \dfrac{2x - 1}{4}$

5. $\dfrac{x + 3}{3} = \dfrac{6}{x}$

6. $\dfrac{x + 3}{5} = \dfrac{x - 2}{3}$

7. $\dfrac{-2}{2x - 5} = \dfrac{5}{3x + 1}$

8. $\dfrac{x + 3}{x - 1} = \dfrac{x + 4}{x - 5}$

9. $\dfrac{x + 2}{10} = \dfrac{x}{x + 3}$

10. $\dfrac{x - 4}{3x + 4} = \dfrac{-1}{x + 3}$

11. $\dfrac{1}{x + 1} = \dfrac{x - 2}{3x - 5}$

12. $\dfrac{x + 2}{-(x + 1)} = \dfrac{x - 1}{x + 1}$

In 13–24, solve the equation by multiplying both sides by the least common denominator.

13. $\dfrac{x}{3} - \dfrac{1}{x} = \dfrac{2}{3}$

14. $\dfrac{x}{5} - \dfrac{2}{x} = \dfrac{-3}{5}$

15. $\dfrac{1}{4x} + \dfrac{x}{4} = \dfrac{x}{2}$

16. $\dfrac{16}{t} = t - 6$

17. $2t + 1 = \dfrac{15}{t}$

18. $\dfrac{9}{x + 2} = \dfrac{3}{x + 2} + 2x$

19. $\dfrac{4}{2x + 6} - \dfrac{3}{x + 3} = \dfrac{x}{2}$

20. $\dfrac{10}{4x - 4} = \dfrac{3}{x - 1} + \dfrac{x + 3}{8}$

21. $\dfrac{x}{x + 4} - \dfrac{3}{x - 4} = \dfrac{-22}{x^2 - 16}$

22. $\dfrac{x - 1}{x + 3} + \dfrac{4}{x^2 + 5x + 6} = \dfrac{1}{x + 2}$

23. $\dfrac{2x}{x - 1} = \dfrac{x + 2}{x - 4} - \dfrac{18}{x^2 - 5x + 4}$

24. $2 - \dfrac{x}{(x + 1)^2} = \dfrac{2}{x + 1}$

25. **Field Goal Average** A field goal kicker has made 28 out of 40 attempted field goals so far this season. His field goal average is 0.700. How many consecutive field goals must he make to increase his average to 0.750?

26. **Movie Rental Club** Your membership at a movie rental club costs $5 per year. The charge for members to rent a movie is $1.50. At the end of the year you figured that the average cost per movie (including the membership fee) was $1.60. How many movies did you rent?

27. **Exam Time** You have 60 minutes to take an exam with 20 questions. After you finish the first 10 questions, you realize you must answer the remaining questions twice as fast to finish the exam. How many questions per minute were you answering? How many questions per minute must you now answer to finish on time? Use the following model to help answer the question.

$$\frac{\boxed{10 \text{ Questions}}}{\boxed{\text{Previous Rate}}} + \frac{\boxed{10 \text{ Questions}}}{2 \cdot \boxed{\text{Previous Rate}}} = \boxed{60 \text{ Minutes}}$$

In 1–3, decide whether the graph represents *y* as a function of *x*. Explain your reasoning.

1.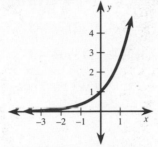

2.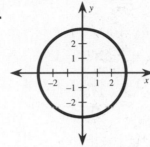

3.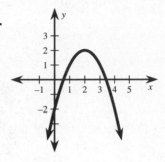

In 4–9, decide whether the information defines a function. If it does, state the domain of a function.

4. {(1, 6), (2, 5), (1, −6), (2, −5)}

5. {(1, 3), (2, 5), (3, 7), (4, 9)}

6. {(2, 4), (3, 8), (4, 16), (5, 32)}

7. {(−3, 2), (−2, 1), (−3, 3), (−1, 1)}

8.

Input Value	0	1	2	0	−1
Output Value	1	3	5	7	−1

9.

Input Value	0	2	4	6	8
Output Value	−6	−3	0	3	6

In 10–21, evaluate the function at the given *x*-values.

Function   *x-Values*

10. $f(x) = 3x + 1$ $x = -3, x = 2$
12. $f(x) = x^2 - 3$ $x = -5, x = 1$
14. $f(x) = x^2 + 3x - 1$ $x = -3, x = 4$
16. $f(x) = 5x^2 + 2$ $x = -3, x = -1$
18. $f(x) = 2x^2 + 8x$ $x = -2, x = 3$
20. $f(x) = 3x^2 - 4x + 11$ $x = 0, x = 5$

Function   *x-Values*

11. $f(x) = 6x - 4$ $x = -1, x = 0$
13. $f(x) = 7x^2 - 3x$ $x = 0, x = 2$
15. $f(x) = x^2 + 8x - 3$ $x = -5, x = -3$
17. $f(x) = x^2 - 4x + 2$ $x = -5, x = 1$
19. $f(x) = 2x^2 + 5x - 3$ $x = -2, x = 0$
21. $f(x) = 5x^2 - 3x - 2$ $x = -4, x = 2$

22. **Record Antler Spreads** The table gives the record antler spreads for five different members of the deer family. Are the given deer a function of the record spread? Why, or why not?

Record (in.) Spread, *x*	74	47.5	33.5	77.625	44
Type of Deer, *y*	Elk	Mule Deer	Whitetail Deer	Moose	Caribou

Profits In 23 and 24, use the following information.

The graph shows the profits of a company from 1984 through 1990.

23. Is the profit a function of the year? Explain.

24. Let $f(t)$ represent the profit in year *t*. Find $f(1988)$.

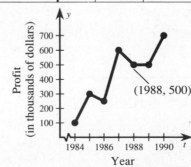

12.2 Name _____

In 1–12, find an equation for the linear function f.

1. $f(3) = -2,\ f(6) = 1$

2. $f(-3) = 4,\ f(-1) = 6$

3. $f(0) = 3,\ f(4) = 11$

4. $f(-1) = 5,\ f(1) = -1$

5. $f(-2) = 4,\ f(4) = 7$

6. $f(1) = -4,\ f(2) = -5$

7. $f(-3) = 4,\ f(3) = 8$

8. $f(2) = 7,\ f(3) = 13$

9. $f(-4) = 2,\ f(8) = -7$

10. $f(-2) = 8,\ f(1) = -7$

11. $f(-2) = -11,\ f(3) = 4$

12. $f(3) = -3,\ f(6) = -4$

In 13–24, sketch the graph of the linear function.

13. $f(x) = 2$

14. $f(x) = x + 4$

15. $f(x) = -x + 2$

16. $f(x) = x - 1$

17. $f(x) = 2x + 1$

18. $f(x) = -4x + 3$

19. $f(x) = 5x - 2$

20. $f(x) = -3x - 1$

21. $f(x) = \frac{1}{3}x - 6$

22. $f(x) = -\frac{1}{2}x + 2$

23. $f(x) = \frac{2}{3}x + 3$

24. $f(x) = -\frac{3}{5}x + 2$

25. *Train Travel* A train travels approximately 920 miles from Chicago, Illinois to Denver, Colorado. The trip takes 9.2 hours. Find a linear function that models the time it takes the train to make a trip. Use the model to estimate the time it would take to travel from Denver to Salt Lake City, Utah (185 miles by train).

26. *Savings* One hundred dollars in a savings account that earns simple interest at an annual rate of 6% will earn $18 interest in 3 years. Find a linear function that models the interest earned. Use the model to find how much interest would be earned if the principle was kept in the account for 7 years.

27. *TV Usage* In 1950, there were approximately 6,000,000 TV sets in use in the United States. By 1970, there were approximately 88,000,000 sets in use. Find a linear function that models the number of sets in use. Use this model to approximate how many TV sets were in use in the United States in 1960.

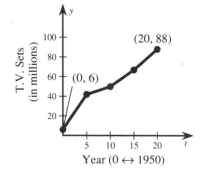

Year (0 ↔ 1950)

28. *Learning Spanish* The table shows the number of students at your high school that took Spanish from 1980 to 1991, where $t = 0$ corresponds to 1980. Construct a scatter plot for the number of students who took Spanish in year t. Find a linear function that approximates the annual enrollment in Spanish classes, $f(t)$.

Year, t	0	1	2	3	4	5
Enrollment, $f(t)$	100	105	110	114	121	125
Year, t	6	7	8	9	10	11
Enrollment, $f(t)$	128	136	142	144	150	154

In 1–6, describe the relationship between the graph of *f* and the graph of *g*.

1. $f(x) = (\frac{1}{3})^x$, $g(x) = (\frac{1}{3})^{x+1}$

2. $f(x) = (4)^x$, $g(x) = 4^x - 2$

3. $f(x) = (\frac{3}{4})^x$, $g(x) = -(\frac{3}{4})^x$

4. $f(x) = (\frac{1}{2})^x$, $g(x) = (\frac{1}{2})^x + 5$

5. $f(x) = 3^x$, $g(x) = 3^{x-2}$

6. $f(x) = (2.5)^x$, $g(x) = (2.5)^{x+3}$

In 7–24, sketch the graph of the function.

7. $f(x) = 2^x + 3$

8. $f(x) = 2^{x-1}$

9. $f(x) = -2^x$

10. $f(x) = 4^{x+3}$

11. $f(x) = -3^x$

12. $f(x) = 3^x - 1$

13. $f(x) = 5^x - 2$

14. $f(x) = -8^x$

15. $f(x) = 3^{x+5}$

16. $f(x) = 5^{x-7}$

17. $f(x) = -(\frac{1}{2})^x$

18. $f(x) = (\frac{1}{2})^x - 4$

19. $f(x) = (\frac{1}{2})^{x-4}$

20. $f(x) = (\frac{1}{3})^x + 6$

21. $f(x) = -(\frac{3}{4})^x$

22. $f(x) = -(\frac{3}{5})^x$

23. $f(x) = (\frac{2}{3})^{x+2}$

24. $f(x) = (\frac{2}{5})^x + 5$

25. ***Body Shop Prices*** Austin's Body Shop claims that they have the lowest prices in town for a complete paint job. In fact, they promise to charge $10 less than any other price in town. From 1980 through 1990, the average price for having your car painted can be modeled by $P(t) = 400(1.02)^t$. Write an exponential function, $A(t)$, that models the average price for having your car painted at Austin's from 1980 through 1990. Graph the function $A(t)$.

26. ***United States and Foreign Business*** The percent of business deals that a company makes with other companies in the United States from 1980 to 1990 can be modeled by $f(t) = 85 - (0.9)^t$ where $t = 0$ corresponds to 1980. Write an exponential function that models the percent of business deals with foreign companies.

27. ***Population*** From 1980 to 1990, the population of a town can be modeled by the function $f(t) = 15(1.01)^{t+1}$, where $f(t)$ is measured in thousands of people and t represents the year with $t = 0$ corresponding to 1980. If this trend continues, estimate the population in 1995.

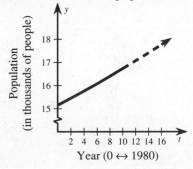

28. ***Salary*** An office worker's starting salary was $10,000. With the cost of living increases, the worker's salary can be modeled by the function $f(t) = 10,000(1.05)^t$, where $t = 0$ corresponds to the worker's first year of employment. Each year, a $100 bonus is available for employees who receive a high evaluation. If the worker gets this bonus each year, write an exponential function, $g(t)$, that models the worker's salary. Graph the function $g(t)$.

In 1–12, sketch the graph of the function.

1. $f(x) = (x+1)^2 - 3$
2. $f(x) = (x+4)^2 + 1$
3. $f(x) = -(x-1)^2 + 4$

4. $f(x) = -(x-2)^2 - 2$
5. $f(x) = (x-3)^2 + 4$
6. $f(x) = (x+6)^2 - 7$

7. $f(x) = (x-5)^2 - 6$
8. $f(x) = -(x+3)^2 + 2$
9. $f(x) = (x-2)^2 - 5$

10. $f(x) = -(x+4)^2 - 3$
11. $f(x) = (x-8)^2 + 9$
12. $f(x) = (x+10)^2 + 3$

In 13–24, write the function in completed square form.

13. $f(x) = x^2 + 2x - 4$
14. $f(x) = x^2 - 10x + 27$
15. $f(x) = x^2 - 4x - 2$

16. $f(x) = x^2 + 12x + 39$
17. $f(x) = -x^2 - 6x - 17$
18. $f(x) = -x^2 + 8x - 6$

19. $f(x) = 2x^2 + 12x + 11$
20. $f(x) = 3x^2 - 12x + 18$
21. $f(x) = 4x^2 - 8x - 4$

22. $f(x) = 2x^2 - 4x - 12$
23. $f(x) = -5x^2 + 20x - 25$
24. $f(x) = 6x^2 + 48x + 90$

25. Coin Toss To determine which team is on offense first, a coin is tossed at the beginning of a football game. The height of the coin, in feet (above ground), can be modeled by the function $h(t) = -16t^2 + 8t + 4$ where t is time in seconds. What was the maximum height of the coin? How long does it take for the coin to reach its maximum height?

26. Seals As part of a show at a water park, two seals play catch with a beach ball. The ball follows the path $h(x) = -\frac{3}{25}x^2 + \frac{6}{5}x + 3$, where $h(x)$ is the height, in feet (above ground), and x is the horizontal distance traveled in feet. Write the function in completed square form. What is the maximum height of the ball?

27. Tunnel The opening of a tunnel can be modeled by the function $h(x) = -\frac{1}{20}x^2 + 2x$, where $h(x)$ is the height, in feet (above the ground), and x is the distance from the bottom left edge of the tunnel opening. Write the function in completed square form. What is the maximum height of the tunnel? What is the width of the tunnel?

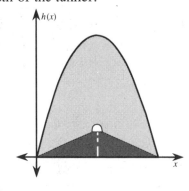

28. Window A stained glass window is to be installed above the main doors of an art museum. The blueprints show the arched edge of the window can be modeled by $h(x) = -\frac{1}{9}x^2 + \frac{80}{9}x - \frac{1465}{9}$, where $h(x)$ is the height, in feet (above the ground), and x is the distance from the bottom left corner of the building. To install the window, how far to the right and how far up from the corner should you place the top (vertex) of the window?

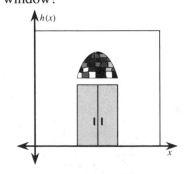

In 1–12, sketch the graph of the function.

1. $f(x) = \dfrac{1}{x+2} + 4$

2. $f(x) = \dfrac{2}{x-1} + 5$

3. $f(x) = \dfrac{1}{x+4} - 1$

4. $f(x) = -\dfrac{1}{x+3} + 3$

5. $f(x) = \dfrac{1}{x-1} - 3$

6. $f(x) = \dfrac{3}{x+1} + 2$

7. $f(x) = \dfrac{1}{x-3} + 2$

8. $f(x) = -\dfrac{2}{x-4} + 7$

9. $f(x) = \dfrac{2}{x+5} - 4$

10. $f(x) = -\dfrac{3}{x+6} - 4$

11. $f(x) = \dfrac{4}{x-3} - 5$

12. $f(x) = -\dfrac{5}{x-2} - 6$

In 13–24, use polynomial division to help sketch the graph of the function.

13. $f(x) = \dfrac{x+3}{x+6}$

14. $f(x) = \dfrac{x-6}{x-1}$

15. $f(x) = \dfrac{x+4}{x-2}$

16. $f(x) = \dfrac{3x-4}{x-3}$

17. $f(x) = \dfrac{2x+6}{x-3}$

18. $f(x) = \dfrac{3x-1}{x-4}$

19. $f(x) = \dfrac{-2x+7}{x-4}$

20. $f(x) = \dfrac{2x-3}{x+4}$

21. $f(x) = \dfrac{5x+2}{x+3}$

22. $f(x) = \dfrac{-3x+2}{x+2}$

23. $f(x) = \dfrac{3x-5}{x+3}$

24. $f(x) = \dfrac{2x+3}{x+4}$

25. *Education* In 1984 you were in first grade. You will graduate from college in 2000. Let t represent the years between 1984 and 2000. The ratio, $f(t)$, of the years you have attended school to the years remaining is given by $f(t) = \dfrac{t-1984}{2000-t}$. Sketch the graph of the function f on the interval $1984 \le t < 2000$. During which year is $f(t)$ equal to 1? What is the significance of this year?

26. *Strawberry Picking* You and your little sister pick strawberries to sell at your family's fruit stand. The first day you pick 25 quarts and your sister picks 15 quarts. Each day for 3 weeks you pick 20 quarts and your sister picks 5 quarts. Create a model that represents the ratio, $f(t)$, of the number of quarts of strawberries you pick to the number of quarts your sister picks. (Let $t = 0$ be the first day.) Sketch $f(t)$.

27. *Geometry* Find the ratio, $f(x)$ of the perimeter of the large rectangle to the perimeter of the small rectangle. Sketch the graph.

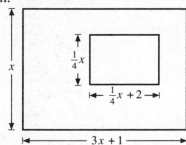

28. *Geometry* Find the ratio, $f(x)$, of the area of the large right triangle to the area of the shaded region. Sketch the graph.

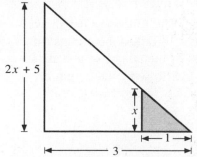

In 1–6, find the median of the collection of numbers.

1. 22, 5, 6, 17, 1, 14, 20, 9, 3, 18

2. 8, 27, 10, 12, 16, 23, 4, 7, 6, 20, 15

3. 210, 242, 216, 230, 249, 248, 215, 235, 239

4. 11, 21, 38, 0, 25, 31, 46, 42, 37, 15

5. 68, 53, 79, 74, 54, 60, 57, 71

6. 4.3, 7.3, 5.3, 6.0, 6.1, 4.9, 5.8

In 7 and 8, construct a stem-and-leaf plot for the data. Use the result to list the data in increasing order.

7. 23, 0, 6, 21, 10, 15, 32, 51, 24, 31, 43, 55, 41, 30, 10, 16, 47, 21, 38, 56, 20

8. 123, 156, 172, 138, 125, 121, 137, 164, 153, 171, 179, 156, 123, 138, 111, 183, 144, 168

In 9 and 10, construct a box-and-whisker plot for the data.

9. 42, 37, 25, 49, 13, 26, 53, 42, 39, 24, 55, 27, 18, 31, 44, 11, 21, 33

10. 123, 156, 137, 144, 127, 136, 151, 142, 153, 112, 147, 126, 133, 127, 135

11. *State Area* The following list shows the 20 states with the largest area (in thousands of square miles). Use a stem-and-leaf plot to write the numbers in descending order of area.

12. *City Populations* The following list shows the 20 United States cities with the largest populations, as of 1989 (in 100,000's of people). Use a stem-and-leaf plot to write the numbers in descending order of population.

Alaska	591	Nevada	111
California	159	New Mexico	122
Colorado	104	North Dakota	71
Idaho	84	Oklahoma	70
Kansas	82	Oregon	97
Michigan	97	South Dakota	77
Minnesota	87	Texas	267
Missouri	70	Utah	85
Montana	147	Washington	68
Nebraska	77	Wyoming	98

Baltimore	7.6	Memphis	6.5
Boston	5.8	Milwaukee	6.0
Chicago	29.9	New York City	73.7
Dallas	10.0	Philadelphia	16.5
Detroit	10.4	Phoenix	9.4
Honolulu	8.5	San Antonio	9.5
Houston	17.1	San Diego	11.0
Indianapolis	7.8	San Francisco	7.5
Jacksonville	6.5	San Jose	7.6
Los Angeles	34.4	Washington, D.C.	6.0

13. *Mountains* The following list shows the world's 14 tallest mountains (in thousands of meters). Use a stem-and-leaf plot to write the height of the mountains in decreasing order.

Aconcagua	7.0	Mt. Damāvand	5.8
Annapurna	8.1	Mt. Everest	8.8
Cotopoxi	5.9	Mt. Godwin Austen (K-2)	8.6
Illampu	6.6	Mt. Logan	6.1
Kanchenjunga	8.6	Mt. Makalu	8.5
Kilimanjaro	5.9	Mt. McKinley	6.2
Lenin	7.1	Orizaba	5.7

© D. C. Heath and Company

1. **Test Grades** The following list gives the percentage grade on a math test for a class of 20 students. Find the mean, median, and mode of the data.

   73, 76, 95, 92, 80, 87, 10, 79, 76, 84, 70, 100, 95, 76, 70, 75, 83, 75, 86, 87

2. **University of Wisconsin** The table below shows the enrollment at the different Wisconsin campuses. Find the mean, median, and mode of enrollments at the University of Wisconsin campuses.

Eu Clair	10,773	Oshkosh	10,881
Green Bay	4,776	Platteville	5,107
Kenosha	5,265	River Falls	5,236
La Crosse	8,984	Stevens Point	8,878
Madison	43,695	Superior	2,480
Menomonie	7,322	Whitewater	9,615
Milwaukee	24,857		

3. **Wimbledon** The bar graph shows the number of times a United States man won Wimbledon. Find the mean, median, and mode of the data.

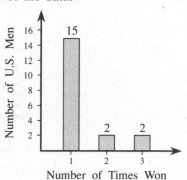

4. **Electoral Votes** The table below shows the number of electoral votes that each state cast in the 1992 Presidential elections. Find the mean, median, and mode of the data.

State	Number of Votes	State	Number of Votes	State	Number of Votes	State	Number of Votes
AL	9	IN	12	NE	5	SC	8
AK	3	IA	8	NV	4	SD	3
AZ	7	KS	7	NH	4	TN	11
AR	6	KY	9	NJ	16	TX	29
CA	47	LA	10	NM	5	UT	5
CO	8	ME	4	NY	36	VT	3
CT	8	MD	10	NC	13	VA	12
DE	3	MA	13	ND	3	WA	10
FL	21	MI	20	OH	23	WV	6
GA	12	MN	10	OK	8	WI	11
HI	4	MS	7	OR	7	WY	3
ID	4	MO	11	PA	25		
IL	24	MT	4	RI	4		

© D.C. Heath and Company

In 1–12, find the distance between the two points. Round the result, if necessary, to two decimal places.

1. $(-2, -1), (2, 2)$ **2.** $(3, -6), (8, 6)$ **3.** $(3, 4), (2, 6)$

4. $(5, -4), (-2, -3)$ **5.** $(-2, -6), (-3, 4)$ **6.** $(4, -1), (5, 8)$

7. $(8, -2), (-3, 4)$ **8.** $(-1, -4), (-2, -5)$ **9.** $(-2, 3), (1, 5)$

10. $(-5, 2), (-4, 4)$ **11.** $(0, 3), (8, 0)$ **12.** $(3, -4), (1, -1)$

In 13–18, decide whether the three points are vertices of a right triangle.

13. $(3, 5), (-2, 4), (2, 10)$ **14.** $(-4, -2), (-3, 2), (1, 6)$ **15.** $(-4, 1), (3, -2), (6, 5)$

16. $(4, -2), (3, 5), (-1, 0)$ **17.** $(1, 2), (-3, 6), (1, -5)$ **18.** $(-3, -2), (3, 4), (-8, 3)$

In 19–30, find the midpoint between the two points.

19. $(4, 6), (2, 8)$ **20.** $(7, 1), (3, -5)$ **21.** $(-3, -6), (-1, -4)$

22. $(8, -5), (4, -3)$ **23.** $(0, 8), (-6, 4)$ **24.** $(3, 1), (-5, 4)$

25. $(-3, 1), (-5, 2)$ **26.** $(6, 3), (-1, -5)$ **27.** $(-2, 7), (-1, -8)$

28. $(-1, 2), (6, 1)$ **29.** $(-4, 3), (-1, 6)$ **30.** $(-5, -4), (2, -7)$

31. *Hockey* A hockey player made a goal from the blue line. When he took the shot, he was on the blue line 10 feet from the center of the rink and the puck crossed the goal line at the center. How far did the puck travel?

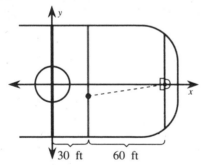

30 ft   60 ft

32. *Distance on a Map* Each square on the grid superimposed on the map represents 80 miles by 80 miles. Use the map to estimate the distance from Honolulu to Hilo.

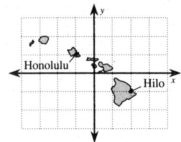

Honolulu

Hilo

33. *Sales* Use the midpoint formula to estimate the sales of a company in 1985, given the sales in 1980 and 1990. Assume the sales followed a linear pattern.

Year	1980	1990
Sales	$620,000	$830,000

34. *Rhombus* A rhombus is a figure with two pairs of parallel sides all of equal length. Sketch the rhombus whose vertices are $(1, 0), (6, 0), (5, 3)$, and $(10, 3)$. Find the midpoint of each diagonal. What do you notice about these midpoints?

In 1–12, simplify the radical expression.

1. $\sqrt{80}$

2. $\sqrt{98}$

3. $\sqrt{54}$

4. $\sqrt{\frac{16}{25}}$

5. $3\sqrt{\frac{1}{9}}$

6. $\sqrt{\frac{3}{25}}$

7. $\sqrt{\frac{20}{49}}$

8. $2\sqrt{\frac{18}{36}}$

9. $\sqrt{\frac{4}{8}}$

10. $\sqrt{\frac{64}{18}}$

11. $5\sqrt{\frac{1}{3}}$

12. $\sqrt{\frac{8}{27}}$

In 13–24, perform the indicated operation and simplify your result.

13. $\sqrt{6} \cdot \sqrt{3}$

14. $\sqrt{14} \cdot \sqrt{6}$

15. $\sqrt{5} \cdot \sqrt{10}$

16. $(3\sqrt{7})^2$

17. $\left(\frac{1}{3}\sqrt{5}\right)^2$

18. $(2\sqrt{10})^2$

19. $\left(\frac{3}{4}\sqrt{8}\right)^2$

20. $\frac{5}{\sqrt{3}}$

21. $\frac{8}{\sqrt{2}}$

22. $\frac{\sqrt{3}}{\sqrt{5}}$

23. $\frac{1}{\sqrt{20}}$

24. $\frac{3\sqrt{6}}{\sqrt{3}}$

Geometry **In 25–27, find the area of the figure. Give both the exact answer in simplified form and a decimal approximation rounded to two decimal places. For approximations, use $\pi \approx 3.14$.**

25.

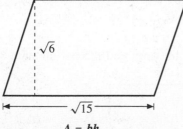

$\sqrt{6}$

$\sqrt{15}$

$A = bh$

26.

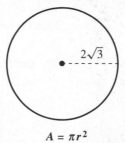

$2\sqrt{3}$

$A = \pi r^2$

27.

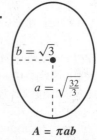

$b = \sqrt{3}$

$a = \sqrt{\frac{32}{3}}$

$A = \pi ab$

28. **TV Screen** The size of a television screen is usually described in terms of the length of the diagonal. What is the length of the diagonal of a screen with length 16 in. and width 13 in.?

13 in.

16 in.

29. **Young's Modulus** Young's Modulus is a measure of flexibility. The smaller Young's Modulus, the more flexible the material. The strength-to-weight efficiency of a column is $\frac{1}{d}\sqrt{E}$ where d is the density of the material (in grams per cm^3) and E is Young's Modulus. Find the strength-to-weight efficiency of each of the given columns of materials.

Steel: $E = 210,000$ and $d = \frac{39}{5}$.
Brick: $E = 21,000$ and $d = 3$.
Concrete: $E = 15,000$ and $d = \frac{5}{2}$.
Spruce: $E = 10,000$ and $d = \frac{7}{20}$.

In 1–12, simplify the radical expression.

1. $4\sqrt{3} + 2\sqrt{3}$

2. $8\sqrt{5} + \sqrt{5}$

3. $7\sqrt{2} - 3\sqrt{2}$

4. $10\sqrt{6} - 13\sqrt{6}$

5. $\sqrt{20} + \sqrt{5}$

6. $\sqrt{48} - 3\sqrt{12}$

7. $\sqrt{18} + \sqrt{32}$

8. $\sqrt{12} - \sqrt{48} + \sqrt{3}$

9. $2\sqrt{8} - \sqrt{98} + \sqrt{72}$

10. $\sqrt{28} - 3\sqrt{7} + \sqrt{63}$

11. $\sqrt{200} - \sqrt{242} - \sqrt{2}$

12. $\sqrt{40} + \sqrt{90} - \sqrt{1000}$

In 13–24, simplify the expression.

13. $\sqrt{2}(3\sqrt{2} + \sqrt{5})$

14. $\sqrt{7}(3\sqrt{5} - \sqrt{20})$

15. $\sqrt{6}(2\sqrt{3} - 4\sqrt{2})$

16. $(\sqrt{3} + 2)^2$

17. $(4 - \sqrt{5})^2$

18. $(3\sqrt{2} - 1)^2$

19. $(2\sqrt{3} + \sqrt{5})^2$

20. $(3 - \sqrt{11})(3 + \sqrt{11})$

21. $(\sqrt{7} - \sqrt{3})(\sqrt{7} + \sqrt{3})$

22. $(2\sqrt{3} - 1)(\sqrt{3} + 2)$

23. $(5 - 2\sqrt{5})(\sqrt{5} + 1)$

24. $(\sqrt{3} - \sqrt{2})(5\sqrt{2} - 4\sqrt{3})$

In 25–30, decide whether the *x*-value is a solution of the equation.

25. $x^2 + 6x + 2 = 0,\ x = -3 + \sqrt{7}$

26. $2x^2 - 6x + 3 = 0,\ x = 3 + \sqrt{3}$

27. $x^2 - 4x - 6 = 0,\ x = 1 - \sqrt{10}$

28. $x^2 - 8x + 3 = 0,\ x = 4 - \sqrt{13}$

29. $x^2 + 5x - 1 = 0,\ x = -5 - \sqrt{29}$

30. $x^2 + 10x - 2 = 0,\ x = -5 - 3\sqrt{3}$

31. *Science Center* A new science center opens. For the first 10 weeks, the number of people that visit the center can be modeled by $N = \sqrt{5000 + 320t}$ where N is in hundreds of people and $t = 0$ corresponds to week 1. How many people visited the center the opening week? Make a table that shows the number of visitors over the first 10 weeks.

32. *Geometry* Find the area and the perimeter of the rectangle.

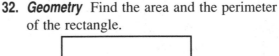
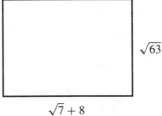

$\sqrt{63}$

$\sqrt{7} + 8$

33. *Scenic View* The railing around a tourist viewing point needs to be replaced. Find the amount of railing needed. (Each unit in the coordinate system corresponds to 3 feet.) The coordinates of the vertices are as follows:

$A = (-2,\ 0),\quad B = (-2,\ 3)$
$C = (-4,\ 4),\quad D = (-3,\ 6)$
$E = (0,\ 8),\quad F = (1,\ 7)$
$G = (3,\ 4),\quad H = (2,\ 3)$
$I = (2,\ 0)$

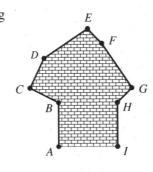

In 1–12, solve the equation.

1. $\sqrt{x} - 5 = 0$

2. $\sqrt{x} + 6 = 0$

3. $\sqrt{5x} - 2 = 3$

4. $\sqrt{3x + 4} + 1 = 11$

5. $\sqrt{9 - x} - 4 = 2$

6. $\sqrt{2x + 1} + 4 = 3$

7. $\sqrt{\frac{1}{3}x + 2} + 3 = 8$

8. $\sqrt{\frac{3}{2}x - 5} - 10 = -8$

9. $5 - \sqrt{4x - 3} = 3$

10. $4 - \sqrt{2x + 3} = 5$

11. $\sqrt{\frac{2}{5}x + 3} - \frac{4}{5} = \frac{2}{5}$

12. $6 + \sqrt{7x + 3} = 6$

In 13–24, solve the equation.

13. $x = \sqrt{12 - x}$

14. $x = \sqrt{2x + 3}$

15. $x = \sqrt{8 - 2x}$

16. $x = \sqrt{-3x - 2}$

17. $x = \sqrt{24 - 5x}$

18. $x = \sqrt{6x - 8}$

19. $x = \sqrt{9x - 14}$

20. $2x = \sqrt{16x - 15}$

21. $2x = \sqrt{-8x - 4}$

22. $4x = \sqrt{2x + 5}$

23. $\frac{1}{2}x = \sqrt{8 - x}$

24. $\frac{1}{2}x = \sqrt{2x - 4}$

25. **Oriental Fan** The area, A, of a portion of a circle bounded by two radii, r, and angle θ, of a sector of a circle are related by the equation $r = \sqrt{\dfrac{2A}{\theta}}$. The length of a side (radius) of an Oriental fan is 12 in. and it opens through the angle $\dfrac{2\pi}{3}$. Find the area of the fully-opened fan.

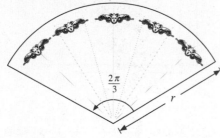

26. **Cylindrical Rod** The radius, r, the height, h, and the surface area, A, of a cylinder are related by the equation $r = \sqrt{\dfrac{A}{2\pi} - rh}$. What is the radius of a rod whose surface area is 50π in.^{2} and height is 24 in.?

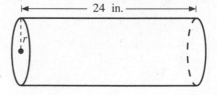

27. **Market Research** A marketing department determines that the price of a magazine subscription and the demand to subscribe are related by the equation $P = 52 - \sqrt{0.0002x + 1}$ where P is the price per subscription and x is the number of subscriptions sold. If the subscription price is set at \$30, how many subscriptions would be sold?

28. **Free-Falling Velocity** The velocity, v, of a free-falling object, the height, h, in which it falls, and the acceleration due to gravity, g (32 feet per second per second), are related by the equation $v = \sqrt{2gh}$. Find the height from which a penny was dropped if it strikes the ground with a velocity of 30 ft/sec.

13.5 Name _____

In 1–3, find tan _A_ and tan _B_.

1.
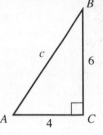

2.
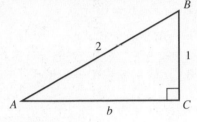

3.
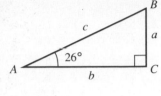

In 4–6, find the remaining side and angle measurements.

4.
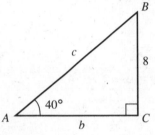

5.
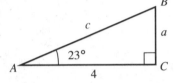

6.
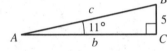

7. **Ladder** A ladder that leans against a house makes a 68° angle with the ground. If the ladder is 4 feet from the base of the house, how high up the house does the ladder reach?

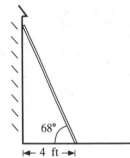

8. **Monument** You are standing 50 feet from the base of a monument. The angle formed by the ground and your line of sight to the top of the monument is 42°. How tall is the monument?

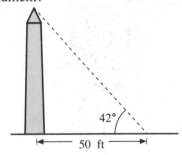

9. **Map Mileage** Kanton is directly east of Weston. Weston is directly north of Audler. Find the distance from Weston to Audler. Find the distance from Audler to Kanton.

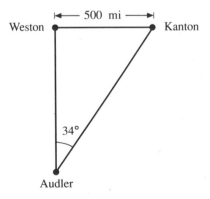

13.6 Name _____

In 1–6, prove the property. Use the basic axioms of algebra and the definition of subtraction.

1. If a, b, c, and d are real numbers, then
   $$a(b + c + d) = ab + ac + ad.$$

2. If a and b are real numbers, then
   $$(a + b)^2 = a^2 + 2ab + b^2.$$

3. If a and b are real numbers, then
   $$(a - b)^2 = a^2 - 2ab + b^2.$$

4. If a is a real number, then $(-1)a = -a$.

5. If a and b are real numbers, then
   $$(-a)(-b) = ab.$$
   (Hint: Use the results from Exercise 4.)

6. If a and b are real numbers, then
   $$(-a)(b) = (a)(-b).$$
   (Hint: Use the results from Exercise 4.)

In 7–10, find a counterexample to show that the statement is not true.

7. If a and b are real numbers, $(a + b)^3 = a^3 + b^3$.

8. If a, b, and c are real numbers, then
   $$(a - b) - c = a - (b - c).$$

9. If a is a real number, $\dfrac{0}{a} = 0$.

10. If a and b are real numbers, $a - b = b - a$.

11. **Distributive Property** Explain how the following diagram could be used to explain the Distributive Property.

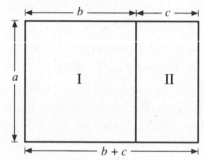

12. **Extension of Distributive Property** Explain how the following diagram could be used to explain the Distributive Property used in Exercise 1.

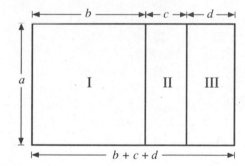

13. **This is Wrong!!** Find the error in the following "proof" of $a(b - c) = (c - b)a$.
$$
\begin{aligned}
a(b - c) &= ab - ac \\
&= ba - ca \\
&= ca - ba \\
&= (c - b)a
\end{aligned}
$$

14. **This is Wrong!!** Find the error in the following "proof" of $0 = -2a$ for all real a.
$$
\begin{aligned}
0 &= a + (-a) \\
&= -a + a \\
&= -(a + a) \\
&= -2a
\end{aligned}
$$

Answers to Exercises

■ Lesson 1.1

1. 9 **2.** 18 **3.** 13 **4.** 4
5. 6 **6.** 9 **7.** 18 **8.** 24
9. 16 **10.** 3 **11.** 5 **12.** 7

13. 6 **14.** 11 **15.** 1 **16.** 22
17. 15 **18.** 5 **19.** 9 **20.** 2
21. 4 **22.** 13 **23.** 3 **24.** 4
25. 18 in. **26.** 20 in. **27.** 12 in. **28.** 16
29. $28 **30.** $0.30

■ Lesson 1.2

1. 9 **2.** 15 **3.** 8 **4.** 23
5. 3 **6.** 13 **7.** 2 **8.** 3
9. 4 **10.** 8 **11.** 1 **12.** 20
13. 0 **14.** 6 **15.** 16 **16.** 30
17. 15 **18.** 17 **19.** 5 **20.** 9
21. 7 **22.** 4 **23.** 10 **24.** 12
25. **a.** $a + b + c + d$
      b. 30 **c.** 21 **d.** 23
26. $2.50 **27.** 32

■ Lesson 1.3

1. 3^4 **2.** 7^2 **3.** x^3 **4.** y^5
5. 3^w **6.** $(6x)^3$ **7.** 4^5 **8.** a^3
9. 2^2 **10.** x^8 **11.** 5^4 **12.** $(3x)^4$
13. 8 **14.** 100 **15.** 3 **16.** 31
17. 5 **18.** 16 **19.** 50 **20.** 11
21. 36 **22.** 27 **23.** 22 **24.** 7
25. $\approx 4.19 \text{ ft}^3$ **26.** 8 ft^3
27. $\approx 75.36 \text{ in.}^3$ **28.** $\approx 28.26 \text{ ft}^2$

■ Lesson 1.4

1. 4 **2.** 7 **3.** 5 **4.** 10
5. 14 **6.** 3 **7.** 11 **8.** 8
9. 9 **10.** 13 **11.** 6 **12.** 2
13. 11 **14.** 3 **15.** 0 **16.** 40
17. 20 **18.** 7 **19.** 8 **20.** 4
21. 23 **22.** 2 **23.** 3 **24.** 1
25. Calculator 1 **26.** Calculator 1
27. Calculator 2 **28.** Calculator 1
29. $\frac{51+50+58}{3}$; 53 ft
30. $17 + 17(0.06)$; $18.02
31. $3 \cdot 4 \cdot 2 + 1 \cdot 3 \cdot 2$; 30 ft^3

■ Lesson 1.5

1. No **2.** No **3.** Yes **4.** No
5. Yes **6.** No **7.** Yes **8.** No
9. Yes

10. What number minus 5 gives 3?; 8

11. What number plus 2 gives 6?; 4

12. What number plus 4 gives 6?; 2

13. What number minus 2 gives 5?; 7

14. What number times 4 gives 20?; 5

15. What number times 3 gives 9?; 3

16. What number divided by 2 gives 3?; 6

17. What number divided by 3 gives 4?; 12

18. What number cubed gives 8?; 2

19. Yes **20.** No **21.** No **22.** No
23. Yes **24.** Yes **25.** No **26.** Yes
27. Yes

28. 8 is the width in inches of a new locker; x is how many new lockers can be installed; 144 is the length in inches of the space available for new lockers

29. 14 is the number of lamps; x is watts in 1 lamp; 14,000 is the total watts

30. 10 is width in miles of crust; 1800 is width in miles of mantle; x is width in miles of outer core; 800 is radius in miles of inner core; 4010 is radius in miles of Earth.

■ Lesson 1.6

1. $x + 4$ **2.** $x - 6$ **3.** $7 - x$
4. $x + 2$ **5.** $5x$ **6.** $\frac{1}{3}x$
7. $\frac{x}{8}$ **8.** $9 + 2x$ **9.** $\frac{x-2}{3}$
10. $3 + 10x$ **11.** $5(x + 1)$ **12.** $\frac{x+5}{2}$
13. $x + 7 = 10$ **14.** $y + 6 = 13$ **15.** $y + 8 \geq 10$
16. $a - 2 = 8$ **17.** $z - 6 < 21$ **18.** $13 - b = 2$
19. $11x = 22$ **20.** $14 < 7x$ **21.** $\frac{a}{2} > 9$
22. $\frac{t}{3} = 9$ **23.** $4b + 1 = 17$ **24.** $6a - 3 = 9$
25. $6 \cdot 10 - 2 \cdot 5$ **26.** $12 \cdot 6 + \frac{1}{2}\pi 3^2$
27. a **28.** a **29.** b **30.** a

Lesson 1.7

1. 70

2. $\boxed{\text{Typing speed}} \cdot \boxed{\text{Time}} = \boxed{\text{Paper length}}$

3. Typing speed = 20 words per minute
   Time = x minutes
   Paper length = 1200 words

4. $20x = 1200$ 5. 60

6. Yes. It will take 60 min to type. The kick-off doesn't start for 70 minutes.

7. $300

8. $\boxed{\text{Price per car}} \cdot \boxed{\text{Number of cars}} = \boxed{\text{Money needed}}$

9. Price per car: 4 dollars
   Number of cars: x cars
   Money needed: 300 dollars

10. $4x = 300$ 11. 75

12. 75   13. $1\frac{1}{2}$

14. $\boxed{\text{Distance to aunt's}} = \boxed{\text{Speed of car}} \cdot \boxed{\text{Time}}$

15. Distance to aunt's: 110 miles
    Speed of car: 55 miles per hour
    Time: x hours

16. $110 = 55x$ 17. 2   18. No. $\frac{1}{2}$ hour late

19. 10 in.

20. $\boxed{\text{Length}} \cdot \boxed{\text{Height}} \cdot \boxed{\text{Width}} = \boxed{\text{Volume}}$

21. Length = 20 inches
    Height = 6 inches
    Width = x inches
    Volume = 960 in.^{3}

22. $20 \cdot 6 \cdot x = 960$ 23. 8

24. Yes, the box is only 8 in. wide and the shelf is 10 in. wide.

Lesson 1.8

1. 12th   2. 10th and 11th   3. Bus
4. 1966   5. 15   6. Elementary

7.

Score	Tally	Frequency
10	||	2
9	||	2
8	⊬⊬ |	6
7	⊬⊬	5
6	|||	3
5		0
4	|	1
3		0
2		0
1	|	1
0		0

8.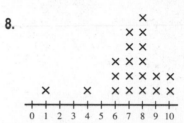

9. 8   10. 2

11.

Hours	Tally	Frequency
7	||	2
6	|	1
5	||	2
4	||||	4
3	⊬⊬ |	6
2	|||	3
1		0
0	||	2

12.

```
              ×
              ×
            × ×
          × × ×
  ×       × × × ×       ×
  ×       × × × × × ×
  +---+---+---+---+---+---+---+
  0   1   2   3   4   5   6   7
```

13. 3 hrs   14. 2   15. 1986   16. 1989
17. 1988   18. 1989

Lesson 2.1

1. 1, 3, 5   2. −2, 0, 4   3. −6, −5, −3

4. −4, 0, 2   5. −1.5, −1, 2.5
6. $-\frac{1}{3}$, $\frac{3}{4}$, 5
7. −2, $-\frac{3}{4}$, $-\frac{1}{2}$ 8. −1.2, 3, 5
9. 1.5, 3.2, 5.4   10. −3, 0, 3.1
11. −2, −1.5, −1   12. −3, −1, 4
13. −5   14. 3   15. −2.1   16. 3.4
17. 17   18. −100   19. 8   20. 4
21. $\frac{1}{2}$ 22. 2.3   23. $\frac{3}{4}$ 24. 1.8
25. July   26. Dec.   27. You   28. Paul
29. 1986   30. 1990

Lesson 2.2

1. 8   2. 6   3. 1   4. −3
5. −2   6. 4   7. −7   8. −6
9. 0   10. 2   11. 0   12. −5
13. 7   14. −8   15. 4   16. 6
17. 5   18. −3   19. 8   20. −3
21. −9   22. −11   23. 3   24. 0
25. $2x + 4$ 26. $x − 3$
27. $4x − 2$ 28. $5x$ 29. $3x + 8$
30. $x + 7$ 31. 18 miles
32. Yes, 11   33. 0   34. Yes, $1500

Lesson 2.3

1. 2   2. 1   3. −2   4. −8
5. −6   6. −15   7. 16   8. 12
9. 3   10. −3   11. 2   12. −11
13. 6   14. 2   15. −3   16. 5
17. −1   18. 5   19. −12   20. −5
21. 1   22. 4   23. 7   24. 15
25. −1   26. 11   27. 3   28. 6
29. −2   30. −5   31. 138 points
32. 48.7 million mi
33. −4°, 8°, −5°, 0°, −1°, 4°; 2°
34. 29 ft

Lesson 2.4

1. $\begin{bmatrix} 7 & 4 \\ 4 & 3 \end{bmatrix}$ 2. $\begin{bmatrix} -1 & 1 \\ 4 & 2 \end{bmatrix}$

3. $\begin{bmatrix} 3 & 2 & 2 \\ -1 & 5 & -5 \end{bmatrix}$ 4. $\begin{bmatrix} -7 & 6 & 6 \\ -5 & -3 & 4 \end{bmatrix}$

5. $\begin{bmatrix} -5 & 0 & 1 \\ -2 & -1 & 8 \\ 11 & -2 & 5 \end{bmatrix}$ 6. $\begin{bmatrix} 3 & 7 & 6 \\ -1 & -8 & -3 \\ -2 & 6 & 1 \end{bmatrix}$

7. $\begin{bmatrix} -2 & 1 \\ -3 & 1 \end{bmatrix}$ 8. $\begin{bmatrix} 1 & 1 \\ 7 & -3 \end{bmatrix}$

9. $\begin{bmatrix} -2 & 0 & 3 \\ -11 & -5 & -4 \end{bmatrix}$ 10. $\begin{bmatrix} 2 & -10 & 3 \\ 6 & -5 & 10 \end{bmatrix}$

11. $\begin{bmatrix} 0 & -4 & 0 \\ -5 & 5 & 5 \\ -7 & 16 & -8 \end{bmatrix}$ 12. $\begin{bmatrix} 3 & -4 & -8 \\ -7 & 16 & 9 \\ -10 & -13 & -9 \end{bmatrix}$

13.

	Male	Female
Germ. Shep.	3	2
Husky	1	0
Lab	2	5

14. 6   15. 5

16.

	Wood.	Brass	Perc.
10th	7	10	2
11th	16	7	2
12th	14	19	5

17. 9   18. 38
19. Grant: 9, 10;
    Lincoln: 12, 4;
    Monroe: 10, 6;
    Adams: 9, 10

Lesson 2.5

1. −6   2. −20   3. 12   4. $−8x$
5. $−15x$ 6. $−18x$ 7. −8   8. $9x^2$
9. $−3x^2$ 10. $−21x$ 11. $8x^2$ 12. $−24x$
13. 8   14. −12   15. 5   16. 3
17. −1   18. 14   19. −24   20. −2
21. 9   22. 7   23. −3   24. −6
25. $x − 2 \cdot 3$; 69 lb per in.^{2}
26. $W − 10 \cdot 7$; 930 ft^3
27. b; 400   28. a; 6

Lesson 2.6

1. $3x + 6$ 2. $4x + 20$ 3. $21 − 7x$
4. $−6x − 24$ 5. $−24 + 3x$ 6. $−2x + 10$
7. $5x − x^2$ 8. $3x + x^2$ 9. $32x − 16$
10. $2x^2 − x$ 11. $−3x^2 − 2x$ 12. $−24x^2 + 4x$
13. $x + 4$ 14. $2x + 7$ 15. $7x^2 − 5$
16. $4x + 3$ 17. $4x − 3$ 18. $−2x − 12$
19. $4x − 4$ 20. $−x^2 + 6x$ 21. $x^2 + 2x$
22. $3x^2 − 5x$ 23. −3   24. $−2x^2 + 3x$
25. $3x − 5$ 26. $4x + 6$
27. $5x − 5 \cdot 3 = 5(x − 3)$
28. $6x + 30$; $6x + 60$
29. a and e   30. b and f

Lesson 2.7

1. 2   2. 8   3. 12   4. 21
5. 20   6. 12   7. −10   8. −3
9. −15   10. $−\frac{10}{3}$ 11. $\frac{1}{28}$ 12. $−\frac{x}{12}$
13. 5   14. 4   15. −2   16. 6
17. 0   18. 2   19. −3   20. 2
21. −18   22. $−\frac{1}{4}$ 23. 1   24. −15
25. 3   26. 550 waves per sec
27. 12   28. 15.75 in.^{2}
29. 6   30. 2 in.

Lesson 2.8

1. $2.50 per hr **2.** $5
3. $625 **4.** 82 points per test
5. 15¢; 12.5¢ **6.** 8 **7.** 2.4 in.
8. $\frac{22}{9}$ **9.** $\frac{7}{2}$ **10.** $\frac{2}{1}$
11. $16.49; 51¢ **12.** $4, the series
13. Sunnyside Center: $\frac{1}{5}$, Westside Day Care: $\frac{1}{6}$, Little Ones Day Care: $\frac{1}{4}$
14. Little Ones Day Care **15.** $\frac{1}{4}$

Lesson 3.1

1. 12 **2.** 9 **3.** 3 **4.** 1
5. 7 **6.** −11 **7.** −4 **8.** 15
9. −7 **10.** −4 **11.** 3 **12.** 0
13. 3 **14.** −8 **15.** −2 **16.** 6
17. 20 **18.** −8 **19.** $-\frac{1}{3}$ **20.** $-\frac{1}{2}$
21. $\frac{1}{5}$ **22.** 12 **23.** $\frac{1}{2}$ **24.** −3
25. $\frac{5}{2}$ **26.** $\frac{5}{3}$ **27.** 3 ft
28. 6 **29.** 8 hr

Lesson 3.2

1. 4 **2.** 3 **3.** 5 **4.** −14
5. 6 **6.** $-\frac{7}{2}$ **7.** −2 **8.** −4
9. −1 **10.** 12 **11.** 2 **12.** 1
13. 1 **14.** 3 **15.** 20 **16.** −2
17. 5 **18.** −3 **19.** 3 **20.** −1
21. −5 **22.** −3 **23.** 4 **24.** $-\frac{1}{4}$
25. 5 **26.** 300
27. 17 ft **28.** 5 in.

Lesson 3.3

1. 5 **2.** 10 **3.** 2 **4.** −3
5. −7 **6.** −6 **7.** $\frac{1}{2}$ **8.** 7
9. −1 **10.** −2 **11.** 11 **12.** $-\frac{1}{5}$
13. 8 **14.** 1 **15.** 0 **16.** 5
17. −2 **18.** 3 **19.** −3 **20.** −4
21. −14 **22.** −2 **23.** 6 **24.** −4
25. 12 ft **26.** 3 g **27.** 11 hr **28.** 5

Lesson 3.4

1. ⌐Left and right margins⌐ + 2 · ⌐Space between pictures⌐ + 3 · ⌐Width of picture⌐ = ⌐Page width⌐

2. $3\frac{1}{2} + 2 \cdot \frac{1}{4} + 3x = 8\frac{1}{2}$ **3.** $1\frac{1}{2}, 1\frac{1}{2}$ in.

4. 3 · ⌐Width of windows⌐ + 2 · ⌐Space between windows⌐ + 2 · ⌐Space between windows and edge⌐ = ⌐Width of house⌐

5. $3 \cdot 3 + 2x + 2 \cdot 4 = 33$ **6.** 8, 8 ft

7. ⌐Width of flag⌐ = ⌐Width of white stripe⌐ + ⌐Width of red stripe⌐

8. $\frac{3}{4} \cdot 48 = 12 + r$ **9.** 24, 24 in.

10. ⌐Width of tape⌐ · ⌐Number of tapes⌐ = ⌐Number of rows⌐ · ⌐Width of box⌐

11. $\frac{5}{8}t = 2 \cdot 10$ **12.** 32, 32

13. ⌐1990 population of Nevada⌐ + ⌐Nevada population increase⌐ · ⌐Number of years⌐ = ⌐1990 population of Maine⌐ + ⌐Maine population increase⌐ · ⌐Number of years⌐

14. $1,206,152 + 157,000t = 1,233,223 + 30,000t$
15. ≈ 0.2, 1991

16. 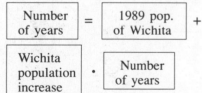 ⌐1989 pop. of Colorado Springs⌐ + ⌐Colorado Springs population increase⌐ · ⌐Number of years⌐ = ⌐1989 pop. of Wichita⌐ + ⌐Wichita population increase⌐ · ⌐Number of years⌐

17. $284,482 + 5500t = 297,391 + 4700t$
18. ≈ 16.1, 2006

Lesson 3.5

1. 2.67 **2.** 1.29 **3.** 3.75 **4.** 0.17
5. −2.63 **6.** −12.33 **7.** −11.8
8. 5.62 **9.** 0.34 **10.** 8.33 **11.** −0.88
12. −4.33 **13.** 1.96 **14.** 1.69 **15.** −0.16

Lesson 3.5 (continued)

16. -0.47 **17.** 0.90 **18.** 6.56 **19.** -0.88
20. -31.2 **21.** -1.82 **22.** 0.84 **23.** 10.96
24. -1.12 **25.** $\$74.72$ **26.** 19.8 sec
27. ≈ 2.58 **28.** ≈ 0.74

Lesson 3.6

1. $W = \frac{A}{L}$ **2.** $r = \frac{C}{2\pi}$ **3.** $h = \frac{3V}{\pi r^2}$

4. $s = \frac{P}{4}$ **5.** $r = \frac{d}{t}$ **6.** $R = \frac{E}{I}$

7. $C = \frac{5}{9}(F - 32)$ **8.** $C = R - P$

9. $s = \frac{P}{3}$ **10.** $L = \frac{s-2WH}{2W+2H}$

11. $v = wr$ **12.** $r = \frac{s}{\theta}$ **13.** 160 ft

14. 10 cm **15.** 12 yd by 12 yd

16. 10 ft **17.** 13 in.

Lesson 3.7

1. $A : (5, 1)$, $B : (0, 4)$, $C : (-3, -2)$,
$D : (0, 0)$

2. $A : (4, -5)$, $B : (-1, 3)$, $C : (0, -2)$,
$D : (1, 1)$

3. $A : (-4, 0)$, $B : (2, 3)$, $C : (1, -1)$,
$D : (-3, -5)$

4.

5.

6.

7.

8.

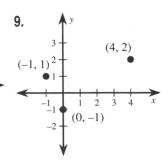

9.

10.

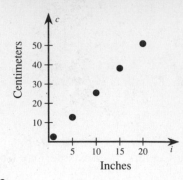

11. 1922

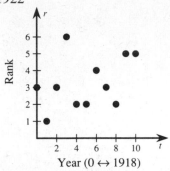

12. July had the greatest profit, February and
March the least.

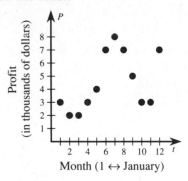

13.

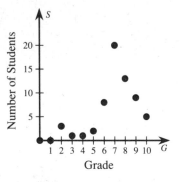

■ Lesson 4.1

1.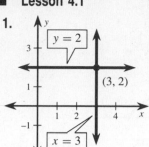

2.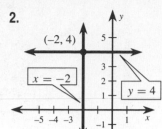

3.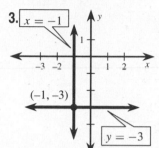

4.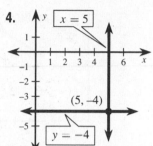

5.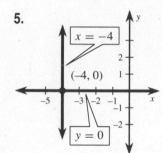

6.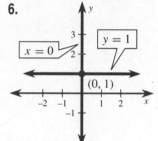

7.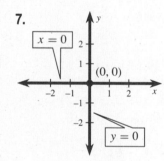

8.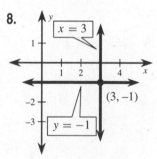

9.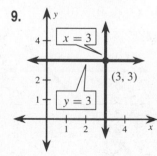

10.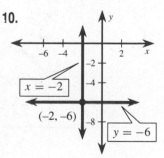

11.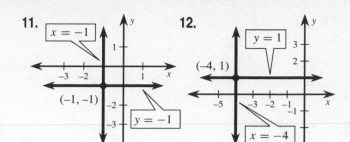

12.

13. $x = 7;\ y = 2$ **14.** $x = 3;\ y = 10$
15. $x = -6,\ y = 4$ **16.** $x = -1,\ y = 12$
17. $x = 3;\ y = -2$ **18.** $x = 5;\ y = -9$
19. $x = -11;\ y = -4$ **20.** $x = -4;\ y = -7$
21. $x = 0;\ y = -5$ **22.** $x - 0;\ y = 8$
23. $x = 6;\ y = 0$ **24.** $x = -8;\ y = 0$

25. 4:00–5:00　Babysat 2 children.
5:00–6:00　Babysat 3 children.
6:00–6:30　Babysat no children.
6:30–8:00　Babysat 4 children.
8:00–9:00　Babysat 1 child.

26. Yes; 6:00 P.M.–6:30 P.M.　**27.** 4

28. All ratios are approximately 0.2, so a model is $y = 0.2$.

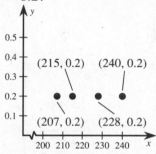

29. All ratios are approximately 0.05, so a model is $y = 0.05$.

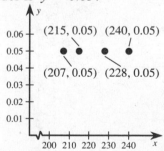

■ Lesson 4.2

1. a　**2. b**　**3. b**　**4. a**
5. b　**6. a**　**7. b**　**8. b**
9. a　**10. a**　**11. b**　**12. a**

13.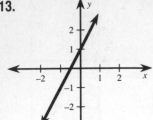

14.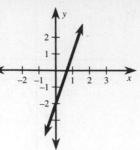

25.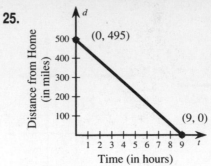

26. 165 mi

15.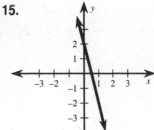

16.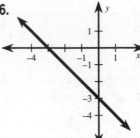

27.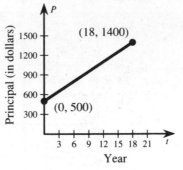

28. $1400

17. **18.**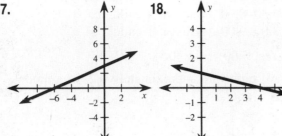

29. $1600

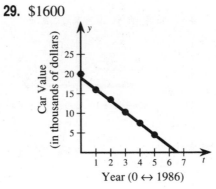

19. **20.**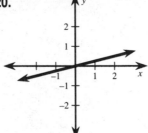

■ **Lesson 4.3**

1. (5, 0), (0, 2) **2.** (4, 0), (0, −3)
3. (−6, 0), (0, 2) **4.** (−3, 0), (0, −1)
5. (−8, 0), (0, 3) **6.** (4, 0), (0, 8)
7. (−18, 0), (0, 2) **8.** (−3, 0), (0, −9)

9. (0, 0) **10.** (2, 0), (0, −6)
11. $(\frac{1}{2}, 0)$, (0, −4) **12.** $(-\frac{1}{3}, 0)$, (0, 2)

21. **22.**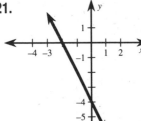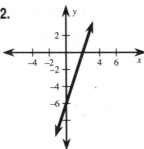

13. **14.**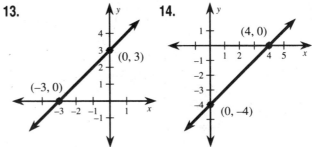

23. **24.**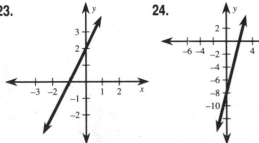

15.

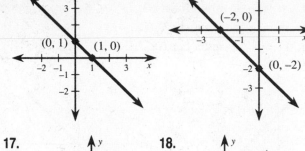

16.

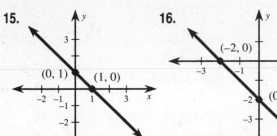

25.

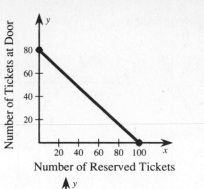

26. 40

17.

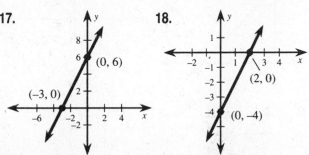

18.

27.

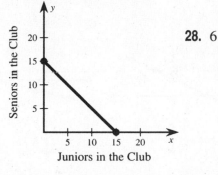

28. 6

19.

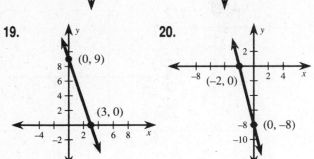

20.

29.

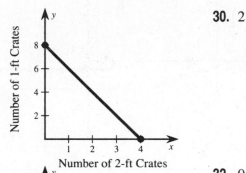

30. 2

21.

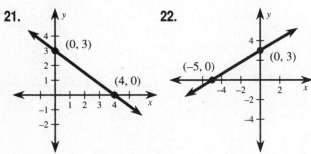

22.

31.

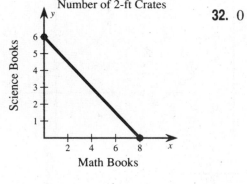

32. 0

23.

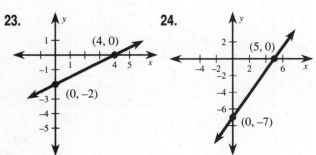

24.

■ **Lesson 4.4**

1.

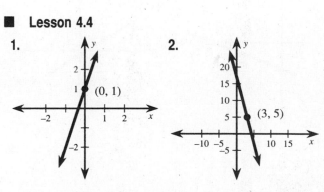

2.

3.
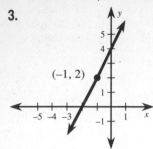
(–1, 2)

4.
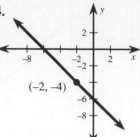
(–2, –4)

5.
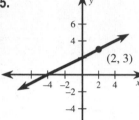
(2, 3)

6.
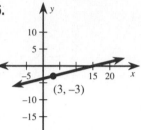
(3, –3)

7.
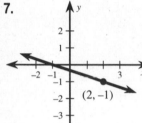
(2, –1)

8.
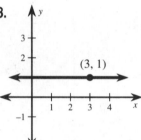
(3, 1)

9.
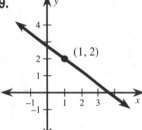
(1, 2)

10.
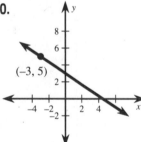
(–3, 5)

11.
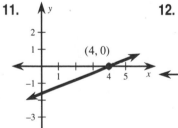
(4, 0)

12.
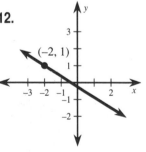
(–2, 1)

13. 4   **14.** 3   **15.** −3   **16.** $\frac{3}{2}$

17. −2   **18.** −4   **19.** 1   **20.** −$\frac{2}{3}$

21. −$\frac{6}{7}$ **22.** −$\frac{5}{9}$ **23.** $\frac{2}{3}$ **24.** −$\frac{5}{2}$

25. 750   **26.** −25   **27.** ≈ −0.17

28. $\frac{4}{3}$ cents per year   **29.** 8630   **30.** 4620

31. 6370   **32.** 1980–1990

■ **Lesson 4.5**

1. $m = 3$; y-intercept $(0, 2)$

2. $m = 5$; y-intercept $(0, -4)$

3. $m = -2$; y-intercept $(0, 3)$

4. $m = -\frac{1}{5}$; y-intercept $(0, 7)$

5. $m = -\frac{1}{3}$; y-intercept $(0, -2)$

6. $m = \frac{1}{2}$; y-intercept $(0, 2)$

7. $y = -x + 5$ **8.** $y = x$
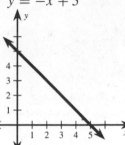

9. $y = -3x - 2$ **10.** $y = -2x + 4$
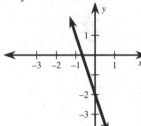
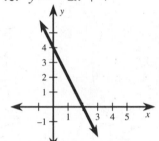

11. $y = -4$ **12.** $y = 2x + 3$
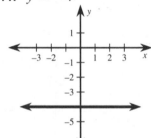
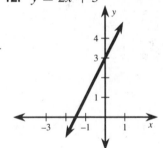

13. $y = \frac{1}{2}x - 3$ **14.** $y = -2x + 3$
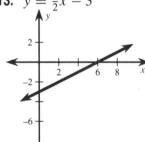
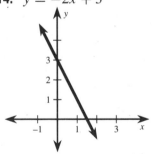

■ **Lesson 4.5 (continued)**

15. $y = \frac{1}{3}x + 1$ **16.** $y = -\frac{1}{3}x - 2$

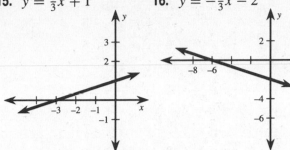

17. $y = -\frac{1}{2}x + 1$ **18.** $y = \frac{1}{2}x - 2$

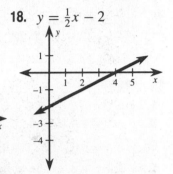

19. No   **20.** No   **21.** Yes   **22.** No
23. No   **24.** Yes   **25.**

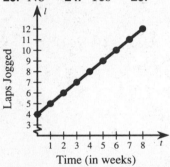

26. 1; number of laps added per week
27. 4; laps Mario originally jogged
28.

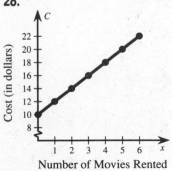

29. 2; cost per movie in dollars
30. 10; membership fee in dollars
31. -1; the wrestler lost an average of 1 lb per week.
32. 190; the wrestler originally weighed 190 lb.

■ **Lesson 4.6**

1. $y = 3x - 5$ **2.** $y = 4x + 6$
3. $y = 7x - 10$ **4.** $y = -2x - 11$
5. $y = 5x + 9$ **6.** $y = -7x + 1$
7. $y = -11x - 2$ **8.** $y = 4x + 1$
9. $y = 3x - 3$ **10.** $y = -8x + 7$
11. $y = -6x - 1$ **12.** $y = -10x + 3$
13. -3 **14.** 4   **15.** 1   **16.** -2
17. 2   **18.** -2
19. 5   **20.** 1
21. $-\frac{1}{3}$ **22.** $\frac{1}{2}$
23. $-\frac{1}{4}$ **24.** $\frac{3}{2}$
25. 10 cm   **26.** 3 in.   **27.** 1985   **28.** 1989
29. 100 mi

■ **Lesson 4.7**

1. $(0, 3)$ **2.** $(0, -5)$ **3.** $(0, 1)$
4. $(-8, 0)$ **5.** $(4, 0)$ **6.** $(-2, 0)$
7. $(3, 10)$ **8.** $(-9, -14)$ **9.** $(1, 2)$
10. $(6, -3)$ **11.** $(-4, 2)$ **12.** $(-7, -1)$

13. 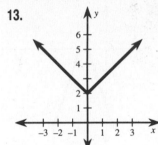   **14.**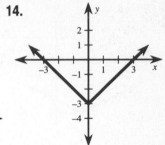

15. 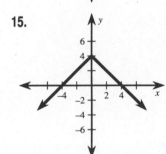   **16.**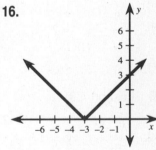

17. 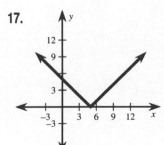   **18.**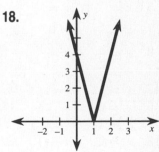

Lesson 4.7 (continued)

19.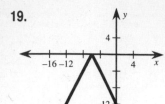

20.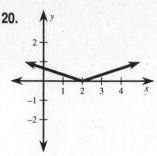

21.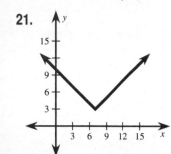

22.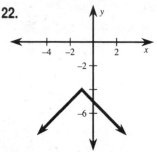

23.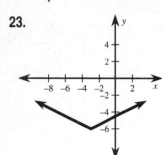

24.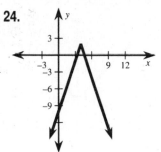

25. a

26. $y = -|x-2| + 2$, $y = |x-6| - 2$, $y = -|x-10| + 2$

27. 3 ft   **28.** Yes

Lesson 4.8

1. $x = 1$, $x = -5$ **2.** $x = 5$, $x = 3$
3. $x = -1$, $x = 13$ **4.** $x = 2$, $x = -4$
5. $x = -\frac{1}{4}$, $x = -\frac{5}{4}$ **6.** $x = 14$, $x = 0$
7. $x = \frac{4}{3}$, $x = 0$ **8.** $x = 20$, $x = -26$
9. $x = 4$, $x = -\frac{16}{3}$ **10.** $x = 4$, $x = -6$
11. $x = 7$, $x = 1$ **12.** $x = 14$, $x = -10$
13. $x = 12$, $x = 2$ **14.** $x = 4$, $x = -10$
15. $x = 6$, $x = -3$ **16.** $x = 1$, $x = -3$
17. $x = 11$, $x = -5$ **18.** $x = 9$, $x = 7$
19. $x = \frac{1}{3}$, $x = -1$ **20.** $x = 2$, $x = -\frac{6}{5}$
21. $x = 6$, $x = 4$ **22.** $x = -1$, $x = -5$
23. $x = 2$, $x = -1$ **24.** $x = 4$, $x = -6$
25. 30 ft   **26.** 100 ft   **27.** 6 ft   **28.** 3 ft
29. 2.5 oz, 3.5 oz, $|x-3| = 0.5$

Lesson 5.1

1. $y = 2x+3$ **2.** $y = 5x$ **3.** $y = 4x-3$
4. $y = -5x + 1$ **5.** $y = -3x - 2$
6. $y = -6x - \frac{3}{5}$ **7.** $y = \frac{1}{2}x - 8$
28. $P \le 42$
8. $y = -\frac{3}{4}x + 9$ **9.** $y = \frac{1}{5}x + 3$
10. $y = -\frac{4}{5}x - 7$ **11.** $y = \frac{1}{3}x + \frac{2}{3}$
12. $y = -\frac{4}{3}x + \frac{7}{8}$ **13.** $y = x + 2$
14. $y = -x + 3$ **15.** $y = 4x + 3$
16. $y = -3x + 5$ **17.** $y = \frac{1}{3}x - 1$
18. $y = -\frac{1}{2}x - 2$ **19.** $y = 0.005x$
20. $\frac{3}{4}$, 7.5, 60, 1000
21. $y = 12x + 50$ **22.** $50, $62, $74, $86, $98

Lesson 5.2

1. $y = 3x - 2$ **2.** $y = -x + 8$
3. $y = 4x + 14$ **4.** $y = -3x + 19$
5. $y = -\frac{1}{3}x - 5$ **6.** $y = -\frac{1}{2}x - 1$
7. $y = 6x + 8$ **8.** $y = 5x + 9$
9. $y = -\frac{1}{2}x - 7$ **10.** $y = 8$
11. $y = 4x + 12$ **12.** $y = \frac{1}{3}x - 7$
13. $y = 2x + 1$ **14.** $y = -3x + 2$
15. $y = -2x - 3$ **16.** $y = \frac{1}{2}x - 5$
17. $y = -5x - 1$ **18.** $y = \frac{1}{4}x - 6$
19. $y = 20t + 210$ **20.** $y = 2x + 18$
21. $y = 0.05x + 15$ **22.** $y = 15t + 55$

Lesson 5.3

1. $y = 2x - 1$ **2.** $y = -3x + 14$
3. $y = -\frac{1}{3}x - 1$ **4.** $y = x + 4$
5. $y = 2x + 4$ **6.** $y = -4x - 3$
7. $y = -3x - 6$ **8.** $y = 3x + 16$
9. $y = 5x + 31$ **10.** $y = -x + 1$
11. $y = \frac{1}{8}x + 6$ **12.** $y = -2x - 15$
13. $y = 2x - 1$ **14.** $y = -\frac{1}{3}x + 2$
15. $y = -3x - 4$ **16.** $y = 4x - 3$
17. $y = \frac{1}{4}x - 2$ **18.** $y = -\frac{3}{2}x + 3$
19. $y = 4x$ **20.** $y = \frac{18}{7}t + 51$
21. $y = -\frac{1}{3}x + \frac{8}{3}$
22. $y = \frac{11}{15}x + 50$, $m = \frac{11}{15}$

Lesson 5.4

1. Yes **2.** No **3.** Yes **4.** $y = x$

5. $y = x - 4$ **6.** $y = -x + 2$

7. $y = 2x + 2$ **8.** $y = -3x - 1$

9. $y = -\frac{1}{2}x - 3$ **10.** $y = 180 - 2x$, 160 lb

11. x represents family size, y represents gallons of milk

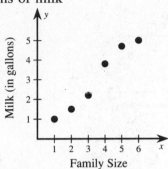

$y = \frac{4}{5}x + \frac{1}{5}$, 5.8 gal

Lesson 5.5

1. $2x - y = 8$ **2.** $6x - 4y = -7$

3. $-3x + y = 2$ **4.** $3x + y = 5$

5. $11x + y = -4$ **6.** $2x - 3y = 5$

7. $-x + 4y = 8$ **8.** $x + 3y = -24$

9. $2x + 3y = 12$ **10.** $-x + 5y = -3$

11. $-3x + 10y = -40$ **12.** $6x + 10y = 90$

13. $-2x + y = -5$ **14.** $4x + y = 9$

15. $-3x + y = 6$

16. $6x + y = -8$ **17.** $-x + 3y = -30$

18. $x + 2y = 6$ **19.** $-3x + y = -7$

20. $3x + y = -1$ **21.** $x + 8y = 17$

22. $-5x + y = 15$ **23.** $-x + 2y = -6$

24. $x + 3y = 12$ **25.** $2x + y = 30$

26. 30, 20, 14, 10, 0

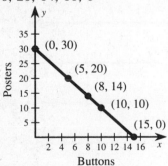

27. $10x + 12y = 240$

28. 20, 15, 10, 5, 0

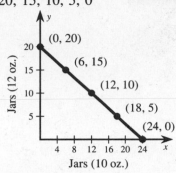

Lesson 5.6

1. $y = 3x - 1$ **2.** $y = -2x + 7$

3. $y = -\frac{1}{2}x$ **4.** $y = -5x - 10$

5. $y = \frac{1}{4}x + 4$ **6.** $y = -2x - 11$

7. $y = x - 5$ **8.** $y = \frac{1}{3}x - 1$

9. $y = -\frac{1}{7}x + 6$ **10.** $y = \frac{1}{8}x + \frac{7}{2}$

11. $y = -\frac{1}{6}x - \frac{3}{2}$ **12.** $y = \frac{2}{3}x + \frac{5}{3}$

13. $y = 2x + 3$ **14.** $y = -3x - 1$

15. $y = \frac{1}{3}x + 1$ **16.** $y = -\frac{1}{2}x + 2$

17. $y = \frac{3}{2}x - 2$ **18.** $y = -\frac{2}{5}x - 3$

19. $y = 0.75x$ **20.** $y = -\frac{1}{2}x + 4$

21. $y = -\frac{1}{2}x + 1250$ **22.** $y = 2x + 10$

Lesson 5.7

1. $y = 0.07x + 1000$ **2.** \$1980

3.

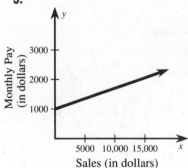

4. 0.07, commission rate

5. 1000, base pay **6.** \$7000

7. $y = 2000x + 25{,}000$ **8.** \$35,000

■ **Lesson 5.7 (continued)**

9.

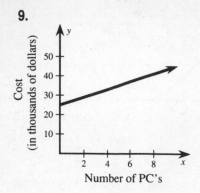

10. 2000, cost of an additional PC per department

11. 25,000, base cost of SPC program   **12.** 7
13. $5x + 4y = 5280$ **14.** 70   **15.** 520
16. $y = -\frac{5}{4}x + 1320$ **17.** $-\frac{5}{4}$ **18.** 1320

■ **Lesson 6.1**

1.

2.

3.

4.

5.

6.   **7.** $x < 3$

8. $x \le -2$ **9.** $x \le 11$ **10.** $x < -2$
11. $x > -4$ **12.** $x \ge -9$ **13.** $x > 5$
14. $x \ge -4$ **15.** $x \le 3$ **16.** $x < 7$
17. $x > -5$ **18.** $x > \frac{2}{3}$ **19.** $x \le -\frac{1}{2}$
20. $x > 1$ **21.** $x \le 2$ **22.** $x < -9$
23. $x \le 1$ **24.** $x < -\frac{1}{2}$
25. $T > 98.6$

26. $A < 15$

27. $T \le -10$

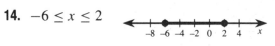

29. $V \le 1000$

30. $m \ge 400$

31. $a \le 50$

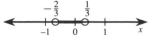

■ **Lesson 6.2**

1. $S < 160,000$ **2.** $h \ge 42$ **3.** $g < 94$
4. $x > 71$ **5.** $r \ge 11$ **6.** $x > 4$
7. 2   **8.** 334 or fewer   **9.** 1982   **10.** 1984

■ **Lesson 6.3**

1. $-2 < x < 2$ **2.** $2 \le x < 5$
3. $7 \le x \le 8$ **4.** $1 < x < 3$
5. $1 < x \le 3$ **6.** $-5 < x \le 5$
7. $-6 < x \le -3$ **8.** $4 \le x \le 7$
9. $-4 < x \le \frac{1}{2}$ **10.** $x \le 3$ or $x \ge 4$
11. $x < -3$ or $x > -1$ **12.** $x < \frac{1}{2}$ or $x \ge 6$
13. $5 < x < 9$

14. $-6 \le x \le 2$

15. $-4 < x < -1$

16. $-3 \le x \le 0$

17. $\frac{1}{2} < x < 7$

18. $-\frac{2}{3} < x < \frac{1}{3}$

© D.C. Heath and Company

Lesson 6.3 (continued)

19. $1 \leq x < 3$

20. $-2 \leq x < 6$

21. $-8 \leq x < -5$

22. $2 < x \leq 10$

23. $-3 < x \leq -2$

24. $0 < x \leq \frac{1}{2}$

25. $45 \leq x \leq 55$
26. $50 \leq x \leq 70, \ 40 \leq y \leq 60$
27. $15 < x < 20$ **28.** $3 \leq x \leq 7, \ 5 \leq d \leq 9$

Lesson 6.4

1. $-7 < x < 3$

2. $x < -13$ or $x > 5$

3. $2 \leq x \leq 4$

4. $x \leq -8$ or $x \geq -6$

5. $-2 < x < 10$

6. $x \leq 4$ or $x \geq 8$

7. $x < 1$ or $x > 3$

8. $x < -3$ or $x > 2$

9. $-2 \leq x \leq 5$

10. $-\frac{3}{2} < x < 4$

11. $-\frac{10}{3} \leq x \leq 2$

12. $x > -\frac{4}{5}$ or $x < -\frac{4}{5}$

13. $|x| \leq 3$ **14.** $|x-2| \leq 4$ **15.** $|x+3| < 2$
16. $|x - 7| < 1$ **17.** $|x + 1| \leq 4$ **18.** $|x + 3| < 3$
19. $|x| \geq 2$ **20.** $|x| > 6$ **21.** $|x| \leq 17$
22. $|x - 3.26| \leq 0.25, \ 3.01 \leq x \leq 3.51$

24. $|x - 100| > 0.01, \ x < 99.99$ or $x > 100.01$

Lesson 6.5

1. No, no   **2.** No, yes   **3.** No, no
4. Yes, no   **5.** Yes, yes   **6.** Yes, yes
7. Yes, no   **8.** No, no   **9.** Yes, no
10. Yes, yes   **11.** No, yes   **12.** No, yes

13.   **14.**

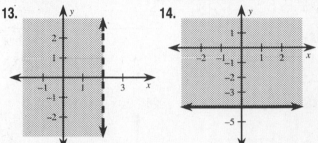

15.   **16.**

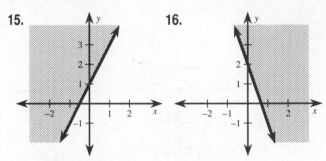

17.   **18.**

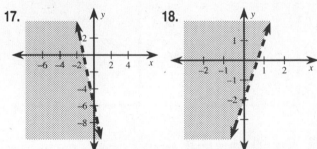

19.   **20.**

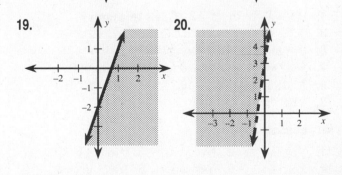

21.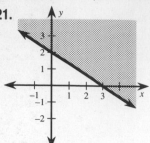

22.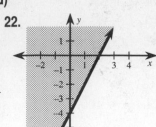

7. **8.**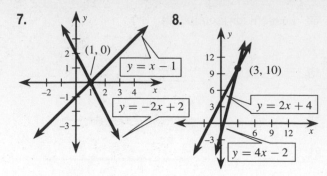

23.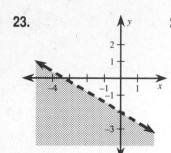

24.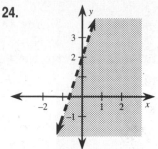

9. **10.**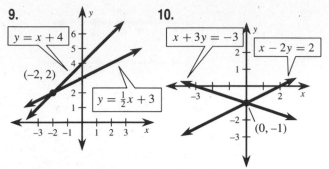

25. $x + y \leq 40$
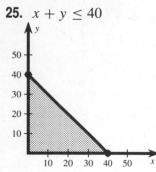

26. $20x + 80y \leq 3000$
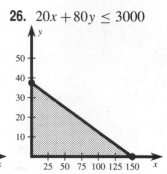

11.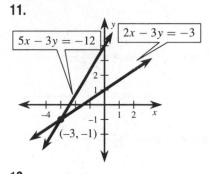

27. $2x + 4y < 28$
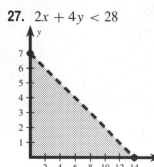

28. $2x + 2y > 16$
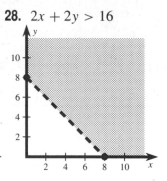

12.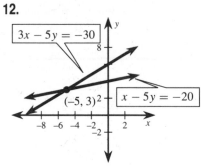

■ **Lesson 6.6**

1. He was born.   2. Class treasurer
3. 3   4. Puppy   5. Piere's
6. Burger Stop and Don's Subs
7. $5,036,200,000   8. $13,559,000,000
9. 15,108,600,000   10. $500   11. $580
12. $20

■ **Lesson 7.1**

1. Yes, no   2. No, yes   3. No, yes
4. Yes, no   5. Yes, no   6. Yes, no

13. Bottles of regular pop = x (bottles)
Bottles of diet pop = y (bottles)
Total number of bottles = 12 (bottles)
Total price = $15.00
6 bottles of regular pop and 6 bottles of diet pop

14. Infielder outs = x (outs)
Outfielder outs = y (outs)
Total outs = 27 (outs)
Number of fly ball outs = 18
18 infielder outs and 9 outfielder outs

Lesson 7.1 (continued)

15. 1986

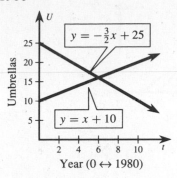

Year (0 ↔ 1980)

Lesson 7.2

1. (2, 4)   **2.** (−1, −2)   **3.** (−5, 7)
4. (1, 5)   **5.** (2, −3)   **6.** (0, −1)
7. (3, −6)   **8.** (−2, −6)   **9.** (1, −3)
10. (3, 0)   **11.** (0, 0)   **12.** (1, −1)
13. (4, −2)   **14.** (2, 1)   **15.** (−3, 2)
16. (2, 3)   **17.** (−1, 4)   **18.** (6, −1)
19. 4 households mowed,
6 households shoveled
20. Mother drove 4 hr, father drove 6 hr
21. $x = 12, y = 4$ **22.** 6 in., 5 in., 5 in.
23. 3 cm, 11 cm

Lesson 7.3

1. (6, −1)   **2.** (14, 3)   **3.** (2, −3)
4. (−2, −1)   **5.** (1, 3)   **6.** (−2, 4)
7. (5, −2)   **8.** (−3, 6)   **9.** (3, 1)
10. (−4, 2)   **11.** (−5, −5)   **12.** (8, 3)
13. (7, −2)   **14.** (−1, 5)   **15.** (−1, −4)
16. (−6, 0)   **17.** (−1, −2)   **18.** (0, 4)
19. 50 milliliters of each
20. 6 tons of 20% mixture, 4 tons of 70% mixture
21. Kicker's distance (no wind) = 40 yards
Wind's distance = 10 yards
22. (20, 10)

Lesson 7.4

1. 9 right-handed, 3 left-handed
2. 5 packages of hotdogs,
3 packages of hamburger
3. Steak: 5 people, chicken: 1 person
4. $w = 4$ in., $l = 6$ in.
5. To the PA-Ohio border: 3 hr
Border to grandparents' house: 2 hr
6. June, 45%
7. $-0.3x + y = 100$

$-0.1x + y = 200$
8. 500 miles   **9.** Company A   **10.** Company B

Lesson 7.5

1. No solution   **2.** No solution
3. Many solutions   **4.** No solution
5. Many solutions   **6.** No solution
7. No solution   **8.** No solution
9. Many solutions   **10.** Many solutions
11. No solution   **12.** No solution
13. $\begin{cases} x - 2y = -6 \\ x - 2y = 2 \end{cases}$ **14.** $\begin{cases} 2x + y = 2 \\ 4x + 2y = 4 \end{cases}$
15. $\begin{cases} x + y = 5 \\ x + y = 1 \end{cases}$
16. No, they are the same equation.
17. $\begin{cases} -50x + y = 50 \\ -50x + y = 25 \end{cases}$
The profit was constant.

23. $|x - 1.2| \le 0.002$, $1,198 \le x \le 1,202$

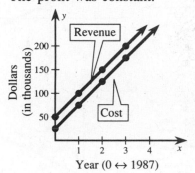

Year (0 ↔ 1987)

Lesson 7.6

1. 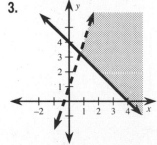   **2.**

3. 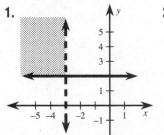   **4.**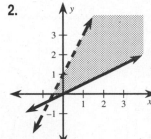

5. 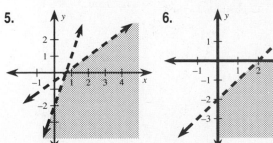   **6.**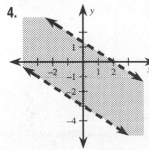

Lesson 7.6 (continued)

7.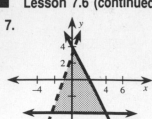

8.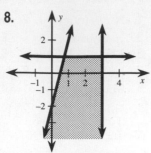

9.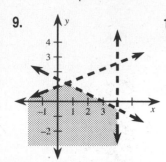

10.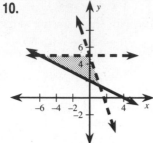

11.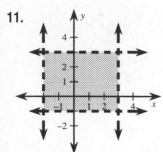

12.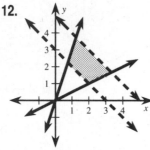

13. $(0, 3)$, $(5, -2)$, $(2, 7)$

14. $(0, -1)$, $(5, 3)$, $(1, 4)$, $(0, 4)$

15. $(-6, 4)$, $(1, 4)$, $(3, 0)$, $(3, -2)$

16. $\begin{cases} x \geq -1 \\ x \leq 3 \\ y \geq -1 \\ y \leq 5 \end{cases}$ **17.** $\begin{cases} y \leq -\frac{1}{2}x + 3 \\ y \geq \frac{1}{3}x - \frac{1}{3} \\ x \geq -2 \end{cases}$

18.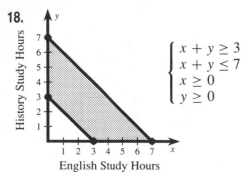

$\begin{cases} x + y \geq 3 \\ x + y \leq 7 \\ x \geq 0 \\ y \geq 0 \end{cases}$

19.

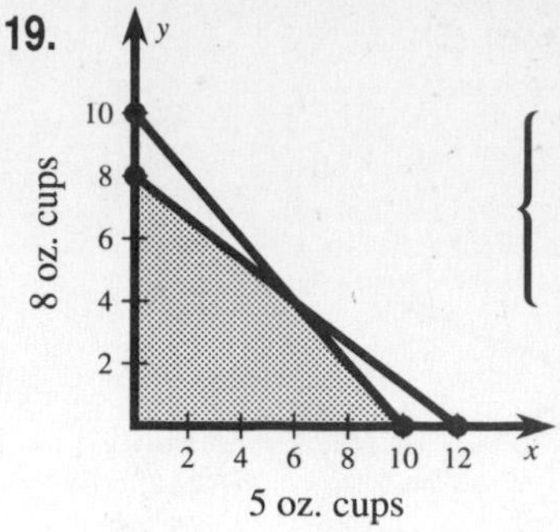

$\begin{cases} 100x + 150y \leq 1200 \\ x + y \leq 10 \\ x \geq 0 \\ y \geq 0 \end{cases}$

(graph with axes labeled "8 oz. cups" and "5 oz. cups")

20. $\begin{cases} y \geq -\frac{1}{3}x + 4 \\ y \leq \phantom{-\frac{1}{3}x +}4 \\ x \leq \phantom{-\frac{1}{3}x +}6 \end{cases}$ **21.** $\begin{cases} y \leq -\frac{1}{3}x + 4 \\ y \geq \frac{1}{3}x \\ x \geq \phantom{-\frac{1}{3}x}0 \end{cases}$

22. $\begin{cases} y \leq \frac{1}{3}x \\ y \geq \phantom{\frac{1}{3}x}0 \\ x \leq \phantom{\frac{1}{3}x}6 \end{cases}$

Lesson 7.7

1. min = 0, max = 15 **2.** min = 0, max = 48

3. min = 10, max = 40 **4.** min = 9, max = 17

5. min = 6, max = 17 **6.** min = 0, max = 12

7. min = 5, max = 26 **8.** min = 12, max = 26

9. min = 3, max = 30 **10.** min = 1, max = 28

11. 10 dozen roses and 50 dozen carnations

12. 8 lake-front homes, 10 regular homes

Lesson 8.1

1. 3^6 or 729 **2.** 2^{15} or 32,768

3. x^8 **4.** y^{16} **5.** $8x^3$ **6.** $9x^8$

7. x^{14} **8.** $8x^5$ **9.** $x^3y^3z^{12}$

10. $a^8b^{10}c^{15}$ **11.** $-x^5y^{10}z^{10}$ **12.** $4x^8y^{13}$

13. x^6, 64 **14.** x^3y^6, 8

15. $3x^3y$, 24 **16.** x^4y^7, 16

17. $-8x^3y^3$, -64 **18.** $72x^2y^3$, 288

19. $5x^2y^7$, 20 **20.** $144y^8$, 144

21. $-432x^3y^6$, -3456 **22.** x^6y^{20}, 64

23. x^4y^5, 16 **24.** $-2x^{11}y^7$, -4096

25. 256 ft^3 **26.** 8π ft^3 **27.** $108.16

28. 1,048,576, no **29.** $(5x)^2$, 1600 mi^2

Lesson 8.2

1. $\frac{1}{27}$ **2.** $\frac{1}{32}$ **3.** 16 **4.** $\frac{1}{8}$

5. 3 **6.** 25 **7.** 1 **8.** $\frac{1}{16}$

9. 8 **10.** $\frac{1}{64}$ **11.** $\frac{1}{36}$ **12.** $-\frac{1}{8}$

13. $\frac{1}{x^8}$ **14.** $\frac{3}{x^5}$ **15.** $\frac{x^2}{7}$

16. $9x^4$ **17.** $\frac{8}{x^7y^8}$ **18.** $\frac{x^4y^3}{6z^5}$

19. $3y^3$ **20.** $\frac{1}{16x^2}$ **21.** $\frac{1}{16x^4}$

22. $27x^3$ **23.** $\frac{1}{y^2}$ **24.** $\frac{3y^5}{4x^2}$

■ Lesson 8.2 (continued)

25. **26.**

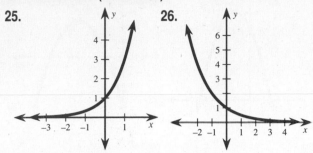

27. 100, 50, 25, 12.5, 6.25, 3.125, 1.5625

28. 1980: $\approx$1206, 1985: 1200
1990: $\approx$1194, 2000: $\approx$1182

29. 10,240 grams

30. 1960: $\approx$1869, 1970: $\approx$1933
1980: 2000, 1990: $\approx$2069

■ Lesson 8.3

1. 49 **2.** $\frac{1}{36}$ **3.** 1 **4.** -1

5. 128 **6.** 16 **7.** $\frac{1}{27}$ **8.** $\frac{8}{27}$

9. $\frac{16}{25}$ **10.** $-\frac{1}{32}$ **11.** $\frac{3}{11}$ **12.** $\frac{4}{9}$

13. $\frac{x^4}{81}$ **14.** x^5 **15.** $\frac{64}{x^6}$

16. $\frac{1}{x^3}$ **17.** x^9 **18.** $4x^3y$

19. $\frac{9y^4}{4x^7}$ **20.** $-\frac{4y^3}{x^3}$ **21.** $\frac{y^4}{x^2}$

22. $\frac{x^3}{3}$ **23.** $\frac{54y^6}{x^{14}}$ **24.** $-\frac{5y^6}{8x^8}$

25. $\frac{3125}{7776}$ **26.** 1.030301

27. 2, 2.4, 2.88, 3.456

28. 100, $\approx$51, $\approx$26, $\approx$13, $\approx$7, $\approx$4, $\approx$2

■ Lesson 8.4

1. 2030 **2.** 34,578 **3.** 64.3 **4.** 720,000

5. 5.2 **6.** 0.0468 **7.** 0.0000013

8. 0.008497 **9.** 0.00098 **10.** 2.5×10^4

11. 3.641×10^1 **12.** 4×10^6

13. 5.642×10^5 **14.** 9.32×10^0

15. 1.5×10^{-1} **16.** 8.3×10^{-3}

17. 7.18×10^{-7} **18.** 6.73×10^{-2}

19. 6×10^{11} **20.** 9×10^{-9}

21. 6×10^2 **22.** 8×10^{-1}

23. 1.2×10^{10} **24.** 3.5×10^{-3}

25. 2.4×10^4 **26.** 3.6×10^{-2}

27. 4.2×10^{-1} **28.** 2.7×10^9

29. 3.125×10^{-4} **30.** 1×10^{12}

31. 1.86×10^5 **32.** 1.2719×10^9

33. 6.681822×10^{-24} **34.** $\approx 2.91 \times 10^{-1}$

■ Lesson 8.5

1. $\approx$8424 people/km^2 **2.** $4000

3. 1.0375×10^3 minutes **4.** $\frac{1}{15}$

5. $\approx 4.684 \times 10^3$ sec **6.** 65

7. 3×10^4 ft^2, $\approx$0.37 dollars/ft^2

8. $\approx 3.26 \times 10^{-15}$ cm^3

■ Lesson 8.6

1. $325.78 **2.** $1191.02 **3. a**

4. a **5.** $P = 100,000(1.015)^t$

6. $T = 4000(1.08)^t$

7. $y = 300 + 30t$, $y = 300(1.062)^t$, yes

8. $y = 500 + 35t$, $y = 500(1.062)^t$, no

■ Lesson 8.7

1. $11,250.00, $1,126.27 **2.** $\approx$50

3. 14,000, $\approx$13,440, $\approx$12,902, $\approx$12,386,
$\approx$11,891, $\approx$11,415, $\approx$10,959, $\approx$10,520,
$\approx$10,099, $\approx$9695, $\approx$9308

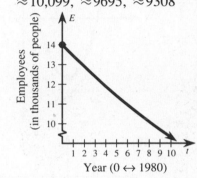

4. $\approx$7.0% **5.** $\approx$5.9 hr, $s = 8(0.985)^t$

6. $v = 600(0.9)^t$, $600, $540, $486, $437.40,
$393.66, $354.29, $318.86, $286.98

7. $\approx$327,291 **8.** $\approx$$1.33 million

■ Lesson 9.1

1. 4 **2.** -8 **3.** $\frac{1}{7}$ **4.** 0.5

5. $\approx$5.66 **6.** -6 **7.** $\frac{2}{5}$ **8.** 12

9. ≈ -10.39 **10.** $-\frac{6}{11}$ **11.** -1.3

12. $\frac{17}{14}$ **13.** 7 **14.** $\approx$3.46 **15.** 5

16. Undefined **17.** $\approx$4.12 **18.** 9

19. $\approx$1.89; $\approx$0.51 **20.** $\approx$2.52; ≈ -1.02

21. ≈ -0.51; ≈ -2.82 **22.** $\approx$5.10; ≈ -0.10

23. ≈ -6.12; ≈ -1.88 **24.** $\approx$0.67; ≈ -1.24

25. 3.5 cm **26.** $\approx$10.05 ft **27.** $\approx$65.80 mi

28. $\approx$17.09 ft

■ Lesson 9.2

1. $\pm$7 **2.** $\pm$8 **3.** $\pm$10 **4.** $\pm$4

5. $\pm$3 **6.** $\pm$6 **7.** $\pm\frac{2}{5}$ **8.** $\pm$1

9. $\pm$9 **10.** $\pm$3 **11.** $\pm$10 **12.** $\pm\frac{11}{2}$

13. $\pm$5.92 **14.** $\pm$3.46 **15.** $\pm$2.24

16. $\pm$5.10 **17.** $\pm$4.12 **18.** $\pm$2.65

■ **Lesson 9.2 (continued)**

19. ±3.32 **20.** ±7.53 **21.** ±1.66
22. ±2.45 **23.** ±6.04 **24.** ±10.95
25. ≈2.36 in. **26.** 18 ft **27.** ≈4.33
28. ≈7.84 **29.** 5 ft **30.** 4

■ **Lesson 9.3**

1. up, (0, 0) **2.** down, (0, 0)
3. up, (0, −1) **4.** up, (−3, −9)
5. down, (0, 8) **6.** down, (−2, 8)
7. up, (−3, −7) **8.** up, (1, 1)
9. up, (2, −14) **10.** down, (1, 1)
11. up, (−1, 3) **12.** down, (2, 1)

13. **14.**

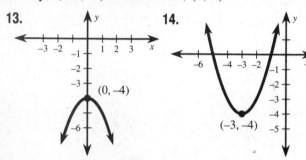

15. **16.**

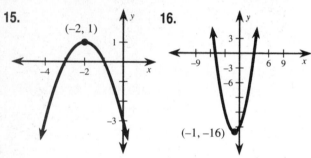

17. **18.**

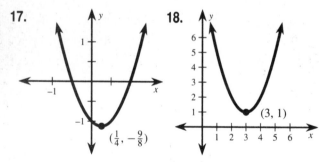

19. **20.**

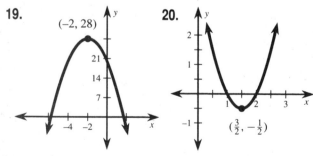

21. **22.**

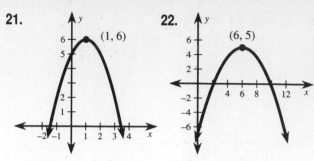

23. **24.**

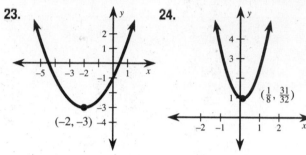

25. 630 ft **26.** 1010 ft **27.** 5 ft **28.** ≈10.3 ft
29. ≈3.89 ft **30.** ≈13.00 ft

■ **Lesson 9.4**

1. 5, 3 **2.** −2, −9 **3.** −2, $\frac{1}{2}$ **4.** 1, $\frac{3}{4}$
5. 0.5, −3.75 **6.** ≈1.19, ≈−4.19
7. ≈6.85, ≈0.15 **8.** ≈−0.28, ≈−2.39
9. ≈−1.59, ≈1.26
10. ≈3.61, ≈−1.11 **11.** ≈1.34, ≈−0.74
12. ≈2.55, ≈0.45 **13.** 2, −4 **14.** −0.5, 3
15. $\frac{3}{2}$, −$\frac{4}{3}$ **16.** None
17. ≈−0.23, ≈−1.43
18. ≈−9.98, ≈−0.02
19. ≈9.16, ≈−0.16
20. ≈0.17, ≈−2.92 **21.** None
22. ≈−0.38, ≈−2.62 **23.** ≈1.26, ≈0.45
24. ≈3.05, ≈−3.72 **25.** 4 in.
26. ≈1.97 sec **27.** ≈0.87 **28.** ≈1.45
29. 1.27

■ **Lesson 9.5**

1. 1 **2.** 2 **3.** 2 **4.** None
5. 2 **6.** 2 **7.** None **8.** 1
9. 1 **10.** 2 **11.** 2 **12.** None
13. No **14.** Yes **15.** 1995 **16.** 20004
15. $81x^2 + 36x + 4$, $(9x + 2)^2$, $6\frac{4}{9}$ in. by $6\frac{4}{9}$ in.
17. No **18.** Yes

■ **Lesson 9.6**

1. No **2.** No **3.** Yes **4.** Yes
5. Yes **6.** No **7.** Yes **8.** No
9. Yes **10.** No **11.** Yes **12.** Yes

■ **Lesson 9.6 (continued)**

13.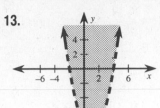

14.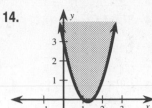

15.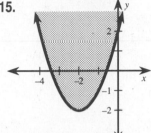

16.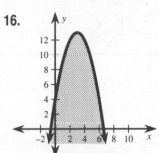

17.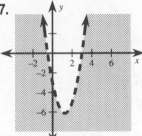

18.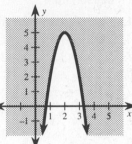

19.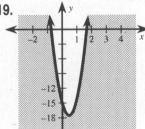

20.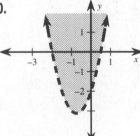

21.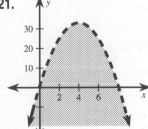

22.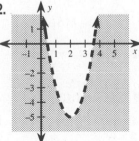

23.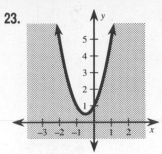

24.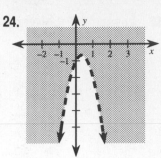

25. No, yes
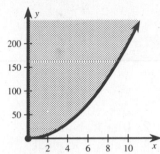

26. Yes
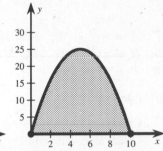

27. 10 cm
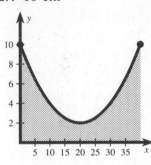

28. Between 0 and 20 meters
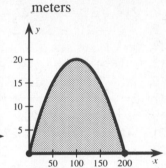

■ **Lesson 9.7**

1. Linear
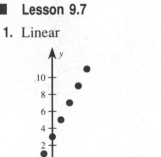

2. Quadratic
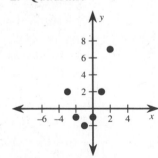

3. Absolute value
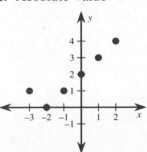

4. Exponential
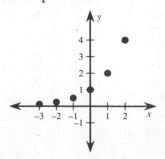

5. Quadratic   **6.** Exponential

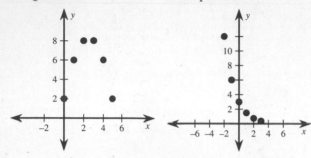

7. $A = 6s^2$ **8.** $B = 100 + 5t$ **9.** $E = 5v^2$
10. $R = 8(1.25)^t$ **11.** $V = 500 - 50t$
12. $P = 10(0.9)^t$

■ **Lesson 10.1**

1. Constant, monomial   **2.** Linear, binomial
3. Quadratic, trinomial   **4.** Cubic, binomial
5. Quartic, binomial   **6.** Quartic, polynomial

7. $2x^2 - 3x - 8$ **8.** $4x^3 + 3x - 1$
9. $-x^3 - 2x^2 - 3x + 2$ **10.** $10x^2 - 3x - 4$
11. $3x^3 + 3x^2 + x - 3$ **12.** $x^5 + 5x^3 + x - 4$
13. $-4x^2 + 6x + 5$ **14.** $-4x^3 - 14x^2 + 3x + 13$
15. $x^3 - 7$ **16.** $10x^2 + 3x + 7$
17. $2x^3 + x^2 - 3x + 4$ **18.** $x^3 + 3x^2 - 7x - 3$
19. $5x^2 - 7x - 1$ **20.** $-4x^3 - 7x^2 + 6x - 13$
21. $-18x^2 - 2x - 5$ **22.** $-2x^3 + x - 8$
23. $3x^2 - 12\pi x + 8\pi$ **24.** $\frac{9}{4}x^2 + 6x - 30$
25. $\frac{4}{15}t^2 + \frac{7}{3}t + 100$ **26.** $0.014t^2 + 0.15t + 10$

■ **Lesson 10.2**

1. $6x^3 - 15x^2 + 3x$ **2.** $-4x^3 + 7x^2$
3. $2x^5 - 4x^4 + 16x^3 - 10x^2$ **4.** $-18x^5 + 6x^3$
5. $18x^2 - 15x^3 + 24x$
6. $-10x^5 - 15x^4 + 35x^3 - 45x^2$
7. $x^2 - 3x - 28$ **8.** $x^2 - x - 30$
9. $x^2 - 12x + 32$ **10.** $3x^2 + 17x + 10$
11. $8x^2 + 5x - 3$ **12.** $5x^2 - 32x + 12$
13. $x^3 + 4x^2 - 3x - 12$ **14.** $x^3 + 9x^2 + 20x$
15. $2x^2 + \frac{29}{2}x + 15$ **16.** $\frac{1}{6}x^2 + x - 12$
17. $2x^2 - \frac{4}{3}x + \frac{1}{6}$ **18.** $6x^2 + 19x + 10$
19. $12x^2 - 20x + 7$ **20.** $40x^2 + x - 6$
21. $12x^2 - 23x - 9$ **22.** $6x^3 + 2x^2 + 12x + 4$
23. $30x^3 + 25x^2 - 12x - 10$
24. $32x^3 - 8x^2 + 12x - 3$
25. $20x^3 + 3x^2 - 9x$ **26.** $14x^3 - 40x^2 - 6x$
27. $3x^3 + 11x^2 - 27x - 35$
28. $2x^4 + 3x^3 - x^2 - 9x - 15$
29. $2x^3 + 3x^2 - 11x + 3$ **30.** $12x^3 - 10x^2 + 8$
31. $6x^2 + 9x - 2$; 2578 ft^2

32. $18x^2 + 30x + 12$; 144 in.^{3}
33. Distance $= \frac{1}{75}x^2 + \frac{1}{2}x + \frac{7}{6}$
34. Total Cost $= 0.25t^3 + 75.5t^2 + 160t + 3000$

■ **Lesson 10.3**

1. $x^2 + 10x + 25$ **2.** $x^2 - 12x + 36$
3. $x^2 + 18x + 81$ **4.** $4x^2 + 4x + 1$
5. $16x^2 - 8x + 1$ **6.** $x^2 + 14x + 49$
7. $x^2 - 4x + 4$ **8.** $9x^2 - 24x + 16$
9. $9x^2 + 48x + 64$ **10.** $x^2 - 6x + 9$
11. $25x^2 - 20x + 4$ **12.** $16x^2 + 40x + 25$
13. $x^2 - 9$ **14.** $x^2 - 49$ **15.** $4x^2 - 1$
16. $16x^2 - 9$ **17.** $9x^2 - 9$ **18.** $25x^2 - 4$
19. $4x^2 - 9$ **20.** $49x^2 - 25$ **21.** $x^2 - y^2$
22. $25x^2 - y^2$ **23.** $x^2 - 16y^2$ **24.** $4x^2 - 9y^2$
25. $8x$, 40 in.^{2}, 48 in.^{2}, 56 in.^{2}
26. $4x + 16$, 36 in.^{2}, 44 in.^{2}, 52 in.^{2}
27. $T = 4t^2 - 9$, \$91,000
28. Brown: 75%, Blue: 25%

■ **Lesson 10.4**

1. $3(x^2 + 6)$ **2.** $6(x - 2)$ **3.** $5(x^2 - 5)$
4. $2(2x + 5)$ **5.** $4(2x^2 + 1)$ **6.** $2x(x + 4)$
7. $7x(x - 3)$ **8.** $3x(2x - 3)$ **9.** $5x(2x + 7)$
10. $2x(10x + 3)$ **11.** $2(x^2 + 2x - 4)$
12. $3(4x^2 - 3x + 5)$ **13.** $(x - 7)(x + 7)$
14. $(x + 6)^2$ **15.** $(2x + 3)^2$
16. $2(2x - 1)^2$ **17.** $(3x - 11)(3x + 11)$
18. $(3x + 1)^2$ **19.** $(x - 8)^2$ **20.** $3(2x - 5)(2x + 5)$
21. $(\frac{1}{3}x - \frac{1}{2})(\frac{1}{3}x + \frac{1}{2})$ **22.** $(5x - 2)^2$
23. $5(x + 2)^2$ **24.** $(7x - 1)^2$
25. $(3x - 5)^2$ **26.** $(5 - x)(9 + x)$
27. $5(5 - x)(x - 1)$
28. $9^2 + 40^2 = 41^2$; $9^2 + 12^2 = 15^2$
29. $10^2 + 24^2 = 26^2$ **30.** $11^2 + 60^2 = 61^2$
31. $A = b_1 h + \frac{1}{2}(b_2 - b_1)h$

$$= h[b_1 + \frac{1}{2}b_2 - \frac{1}{2}b_1]$$

$$= h[\frac{1}{2}b_1 + \frac{1}{2}b_2]$$

$$= \frac{1}{2}h[b_1 + b_2]$$

32. $\pi x^2 - \pi y^2$, $\pi(x - y)(x + y)$, 21π cm^2

■ **Lesson 10.5**

1. $(x + 3)(x + 5)$ **2.** $(x - 4)(x - 1)$
3. $(x - 7)(x + 6)$ **4.** $(x - 2)(x + 8)$
5. $(2x + 1)(x - 3)$ **6.** $(3x - 2)(x + 4)$
7. $(7x - 3)(x - 4)$ **8.** $(5x + 2)(x + 1)$
9. $(2x - 3)(3x - 1)$ **10.** $(5x + 1)(6x - 1)$
11. $(4x - 3)(5x + 2)$ **12.** $(2x + 3)(5x + 1)$
13. Yes, $(4x + 3)(2x - 1)$ **14.** No   **15.** No

Lesson 10.5 (continued)

16. Yes, $4(x + 3)(x - 1)$ **17.** No

18. Yes, $(6x - 1)(2x + 3)$

19. No **20.** No **21.** Yes, $(2 - 3x)(1 - 5x)$

22. Yes, $(3 - 4x)(2 + x)$ **23.** No **24.** No

25. $x + 6$, $x - 2$ **26.** $2x + 1$, $x + 5$

27. $t + 8$; 8, 9, 10, 11, 12, 13

28. $5 + \frac{1}{4}t$; \$5.00, \$5.25, \$5.50, \$5.75, \$6.00

Lesson 10.6

1. -3, 2 **2.** 5, 3 **3.** 1, -4

4. 2, $-\frac{1}{3}$ **5.** 3, $\frac{3}{2}$ **6.** $-\frac{2}{3}$, -1

7. $-\frac{1}{2}$, $-\frac{3}{4}$ **8.** $-\frac{1}{2}$, $\frac{5}{2}$ **9.** $\frac{3}{4}$, $-\frac{1}{3}$

10. $-\frac{5}{3}$, $\frac{3}{5}$ **11.** $\frac{1}{4}$, $\frac{5}{2}$ **12.** $-\frac{1}{3}$, $-\frac{1}{2}$

13. $\frac{3}{2}$, $-\frac{3}{2}$ **14.** 0, -6 **15.** ≈ 3.73, ≈ 0.27

16. 3, 7 **17.** ≈ -7.14, ≈ 0.14

18. ≈ -0.85, ≈ 2.35 **19.** 0, 8

20. -3 **21.** $-\frac{3}{2}$, 2 **22.** $-\frac{1}{3}$, $\frac{1}{4}$

23. $\frac{1}{2}$, -4 **24.** ≈ 0.69, ≈ -2.19

25. $r = 12$ cm **26.** 6 in. $\times$ 10 in.

27. Height = 6 in., base = 9 in. **28.** 1 sec

29. 11 in. $\times$ 5 in. $\times$ 2 in., 15 in. $\times$ 9 in.

30. 10 ft $\times$ 17 ft, 54 ft

Lesson 10.7

1. $-5 \pm \sqrt{29}$ **2.** $-3 \pm \sqrt{10}$ **3.** $4 \pm \sqrt{13}$

4. $3 \pm \sqrt{17}$ **5.** $-6 \pm \sqrt{39}$ **6.** $-2 \pm \sqrt{2}$

7. $5 \pm \sqrt{21}$ **8.** $-4 \pm 2\sqrt{2}$ **9.** $-2 \pm \sqrt{7}$

10. $4 \pm \sqrt{14}$ **11.** $-2 \pm \sqrt{6}$ **12.** $1 \pm \sqrt{5}$

13. 3, 4 **14.** 0, 3 **15.** $\pm\sqrt{5}$

16. $-2 \pm 2\sqrt{2}$ **17.** $\pm\frac{5}{3}$ **18.** $-\frac{3}{2}$, 1

19. $-\frac{4 \pm \sqrt{30}}{2}$ **20.** $-\frac{2 \pm \sqrt{10}}{3}$ **21.** $\frac{1 \pm \sqrt{41}}{10}$

22. $-\frac{1}{3}$, $-\frac{3}{2}$ **23.** $10 \pm 2\sqrt{10}$ **24.** $\frac{7 \pm \sqrt{29}}{2}$

25. 23,328 **26.** ≈ 71.4 mi; ≈ 96.4 mi.

27. 11 ft **28.** $\frac{1}{4}$ mile

Lesson 11.1

1. $\frac{12}{5}$ **2.** $-\frac{5}{2}$ **3.** $\frac{14}{3}$ **4.** $\frac{33}{5}$

5. $-\frac{7}{2}$ **6.** $\frac{3}{14}$ **7.** $-\frac{9}{10}$ **8.** $\frac{1}{2}$

9. $\frac{17}{3}$ **10.** -5, 1 **11.** 0, 3 **12.** 8, -2

13. 3, 6 **14.** -3, 5 **15.** -6, -1

16. 3, 6 **17.** 6, -1 **18.** $-\frac{3}{2}$, 8

19. 11,550 in. or 962.5 ft

20. 453.25 in. or ≈ 37.8 ft **21.** 54 in.

22. 29.7 in. **23.** 0.75 ft or 9 in. **24.** 27

Lesson 11.2

1. 9 **2.** 12% **3.** 600 **4.** 160

5. 120 **6.** 64% **7.** 88% **8.** 80

9. 219 **10.** 138.6 **11.** 44% **12.** 70

13. 50% **14.** $\approx 44\%$

15. $\approx 1.90933 \times 10^8$ square miles

16. $\approx 2.487 \times 10^8$ **17.** ≈ 94 **18.** ≈ 6

19. ≈ 1 **20.** ≈ 4 **21.** 16 **22.** 24

23. 98 **24.** 62

Lesson 11.3

1. $y = 8x$ **2.** $y = \frac{1}{4}x$ **3.** $y = \frac{7}{3}x$

4. $y = \frac{5}{8}x$ **5.** $y = \frac{3}{8}x$ **6.** $y = \frac{3}{2}x$

7. $xy = 21$ **8.** $xy = 10$ **9.** $xy = 24$

10. $xy = 8$ **11.** $xy = 5$ **12.** $xy = \frac{10}{3}$

13. 4 **14.** 10 **15.** 18 **16.** $\frac{6}{5}$

17. $\frac{9}{2}$ **18.** 5 **19.** 3 **20.** $\frac{7}{4}$

21. $\frac{3}{4}$ **22.** 2 **23.** $\frac{4}{3}$ **24.** $\frac{1}{24}$

25. $C = 2\pi r$ **26.** $f \cdot \gamma \approx 2.99 \times 10^5$

27. 6 volts **28.** 4 lb

Lesson 11.4

1. $\frac{1}{6}$ **2.** $\frac{1}{40}$ or 0.025 **3.** $\frac{5}{6}$ **4.** $\frac{6}{11}$

5. 0.000002 **6.** 2,750,000 **7.** $\approx 297,576$

8. $\frac{7}{160}$ **9.** $\frac{7}{44} \approx 0.16$ **10.** $\frac{3}{22} \approx 0.14$

11. $\frac{2}{11} \approx 0.18$ **12.** $\frac{5}{22} \approx 0.23$

13. ≈ 0.086, ≈ 0.059, ≈ 0.048, ≈ 0.035, ≈ 0.026, ≈ 0.021, ≈ 0.015

Lesson 11.5

1. All real numbers except 2

2. All real numbers except -3

3. All real numbers except 0 and 1

4. All real numbers except -4

5. All real numbers except 2 and -2

6. All real numbers except 4 and -4

7. All real numbers except 7 and -7

8. All real numbers except 3 and -3

9. All real numbers except -2 and -1

10. All real numbers except 4 and -3

11. All real numbers except -1 and $\frac{1}{2}$

12. All real numbers except $\frac{2}{3}$ and 4

13. $\frac{x}{3}$ **14.** $\frac{5x}{7}$ **15.** $\frac{3x}{2}$ **16.** $\frac{6}{7x^3}$

17. $\frac{5}{x+3}$ **18.** $\frac{2x+1}{4}$ **19.** $\frac{x-1}{6}$ **20.** $\frac{4}{x+3}$

21. $\frac{x-5}{x+3}$ **22.** $\frac{x+1}{2x-1}$ **23.** $\frac{x+6}{x-4}$ **24.** $\frac{x-4}{x-3}$

25. $\frac{6(t+4)}{18-0.5t+0.01t^2}$ **26.** 600,000

27. $\frac{8t+11}{3-0.2t+0.1t^2}$ **28.** ≈ 8273 lb

29. $\frac{5}{2}x(2x + 3)$, $45x$, $\frac{2x+3}{18}$ **30.** $\frac{x-3}{x-2}$

Lesson 11.6

1. $\frac{8}{3}$ **2.** $\frac{14}{x}$ **3.** $\frac{32x}{15}$ **4.** $\frac{3}{2x^2}$

5. $\frac{3x}{4}$ **6.** $\frac{30}{x-4}$ **7.** $\frac{4(x-7)}{x(x+7)}$

8. $\frac{7x}{2x-1}$ **9.** $\frac{2(x+1)}{(x+3)(x-5)}$

10. $\frac{2(5x+3)}{5x-3}$ **11.** $\frac{x-2}{3x(x-3)}$ **12.** $\frac{x+4}{x-1}$

13. $\frac{x^4}{6}$ **14.** $-\frac{5}{4}$ **15.** $\frac{3}{4x^4}$

16. $\frac{x}{x-1}$ **17.** $-\frac{1}{7}$ **18.** $\frac{8}{x-5}$

19. $\frac{x-2}{x+8}$ **20.** $\frac{1}{8(x-7)}$ **21.** $\frac{2(x-1)}{x+1}$

22. $\frac{x+6}{x+1}$ **23.** $\frac{2x}{3}$ **24.** $\frac{2}{x^2(x-1)}$

25. $\frac{2(10+3t)}{11-t}$ **26.** $\frac{150}{150-t}$ **27.** $2x^2$

■ **Lesson 11.7**

1. $6x-4$ **2.** $\frac{3}{2}x^2+4x-1$

3. $\frac{1}{3}x^2+\frac{4}{3}$ **4.** $7x+5-\frac{2}{x}$ **5.** $x^2+1+\frac{5}{x}$

6. $x^9-\frac{18}{x}$ **7.** $-9x^2-3x+6-\frac{1}{x}$

8. $x+6$ **9.** $8x^2-4x+5+\frac{6}{x}$

10. $3x-2+\frac{5}{2x}$

11. $5x^2+4x-\frac{7}{2}-\frac{1}{2x}$ **12.** $4x^2+2x-1+\frac{1}{2x}$

13. $2-\frac{7}{x+3}$ **14.** $13+\frac{30}{x-2}$ **15.** $2x-4-\frac{1}{x-1}$

16. $x+2-\frac{4}{x-2}$ **17.** $5x+1-\frac{3}{x+3}$

18. $3x+5+\frac{10}{x-5}$

19. $x+8+\frac{26}{x-4}$ **20.** $3-\frac{5}{3x-1}$

21. $5+\frac{3}{2x+5}$ **22.** $5x-\frac{1}{2}+\frac{15}{2(2x+1)}$

23. $2x-1-\frac{1}{2x-3}$ **24.** $6x-3-\frac{2}{4x+1}$

25. $x^2+\frac{3}{2}x$ **26.** $4x+5-\frac{6}{x}$

27. $\frac{1}{4}-\frac{19}{20t+168}$
   $\approx 0.14,\ \approx 0.16,\ \approx 0.17,\ \approx 0.18,\ \approx 0.19,\ \approx 0.20$;
   more

28. $\frac{1}{2}+\frac{5}{t+5}$,
   $1.5,\ \approx 1.2,\ \approx 1.06,\ \approx 0.95,\ \approx 0.88,\ \approx 0.83$; less

■ **Lesson 11.8**

1. $\frac{12}{7}$ **2.** 6 **3.** 6 **4.** $\frac{5}{6}$

5. $3, -6$ **6.** $\frac{19}{2}$ **7.** $\frac{23}{16}$ **8.** $-\frac{11}{5}$

9. $3, 2$ **10.** $-4, 2$ **11.** $3, 1$ **12.** $-\frac{1}{2}$

13. $-1, 3$ **14.** $-5, 2$ **15.** $1, -1$

16. $8, -2$ **17.** $\frac{5}{2}, -3$ **18.** $1, -3$

19. $-1, -2$ **20.** -1 **21.** $2, 5$

22. $-1, 1$ **23.** 5 **24.** $0, -\frac{1}{2}$

25. 8 **26.** 50

27. $\frac{1}{4}$ of a question per minute
   $\frac{1}{2}$ of a question per minute

■ **Lesson 12.1**

1. Yes. No 2 ordered pairs have the same 1st coordinate.

2. No. Two ordered pairs have same 1st coordinate.

3. Yes. No 2 ordered pairs have the same 1st coordinate.

4. No **5.** Yes, {1, 2, 3, 4}

6. Yes, {2, 3, 4, 5}

7. No **8.** No **9.** Yes, {0, 2, 4, 6, 8}

10. $-8, 7$ **11.** $-10, -4$ **12.** $22, -2$

13. $0, 22$ **14.** $-1, 27$ **15.** $-18, -18$

16. $47, 7$ **17.** $47, -1$ **18.** $-8, 42$

19. $-5, -3$ **20.** $11, 66$ **21.** $90, 12$

22. Yes. No 2 ordered pairs have the same 1st coordinate.

23. Yes. No 2 ordered pairs have the same 1st coordinate.

24. $f(1988) = \$500{,}000$

■ **Lesson 12.2**

1. $f(x) = x - 5$ **2.** $f(x) = x + 7$

3. $f(x) = 2x + 3$ **4.** $f(x) = -3x + 2$

5. $f(x) = \frac{1}{2}x + 5$ **6.** $f(x) = -x - 3$

7. $f(x) = \frac{2}{3}x + 6$ **8.** $f(x) = 6x - 5$

9. $f(x) = -\frac{3}{4}x - 1$ **10.** $f(x) = -5x - 2$

11. $f(x) = 3x - 5$ **12.** $f(x) = -\frac{1}{3}x - 2$

13. **14.**

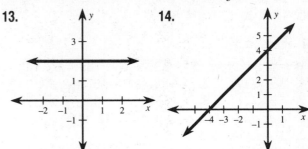

15. **16.**

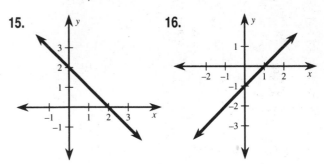

17. **18.**

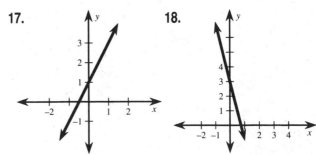

Lesson 12.2 (continued)

19.

20.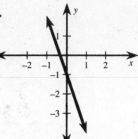

7.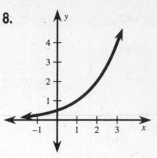

8.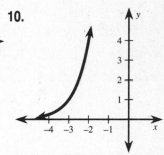

21.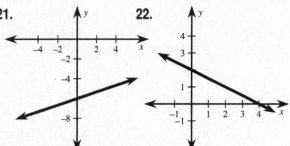

22.

9.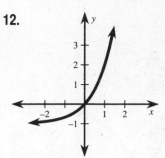

10.

23.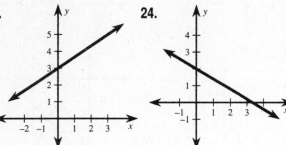

24.

11.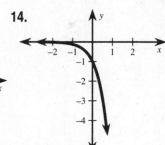

12.

25. $f(m) = \frac{1}{100}m$, 1.85 hr
26. $f(t) = 100 \cdot 0.06t$, \$42
27. $f(t) = 4{,}100{,}000t + 6{,}000{,}000$, 47,000,000

28. $f(t) = 5t + 100$

13.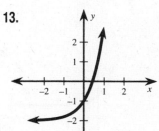

14.

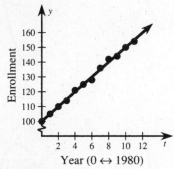
Year (0 ↔ 1980)

15.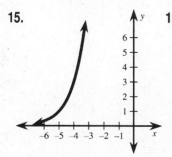

16.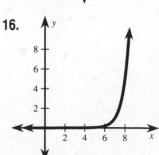

Lesson 12.3

1. g is shifted left 1 unit
2. g is shifted down 2 units
3. g is reflected in the x-axis
4. g is shifted up 5 units
5. g is shifted right 2 units
6. g is shifted left 3 units

■ **Lesson 12.3 (continued)**

17.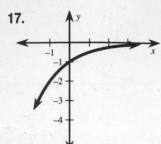

18.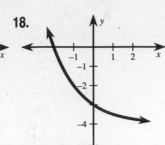

28. $g(t) = 100 + 10,000(1.05)^t$

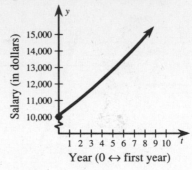

19. **20.**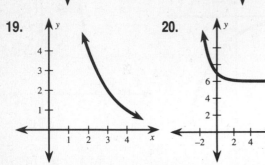

■ **Lesson 12.4**

1. **2.**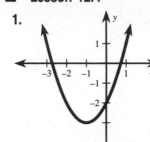

21. **22.**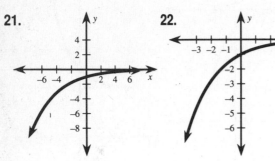

3. **4.**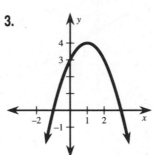

23. **24.**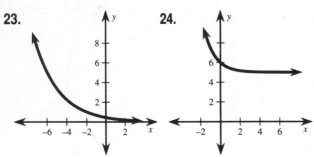

5. **6.**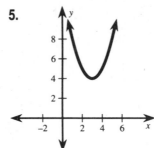

25. $A(t) = 400(1.02)^t - 10$

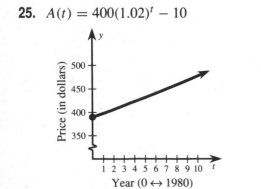

7. **8.**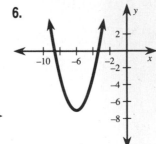

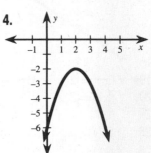

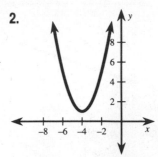

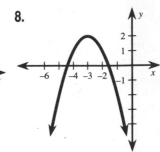

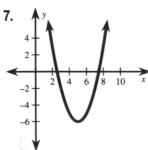

26. $g(t) = 15 + (0.9)^t$ **27.** $\approx 17,600$

■ **Lesson 12.4 (continued)**

9.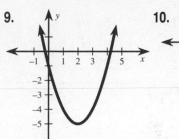

10.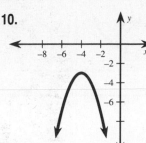

11.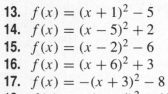

12.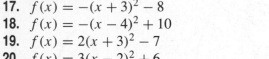

3.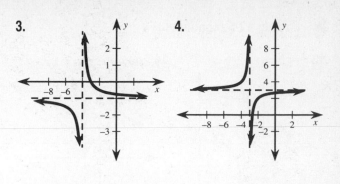

4.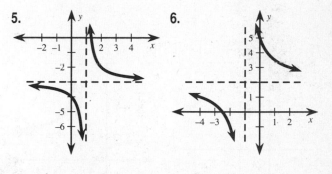

5.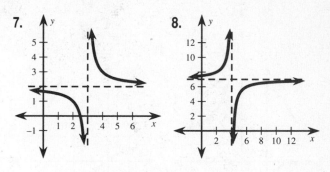

6.

13. $f(x) = (x + 1)^2 - 5$
14. $f(x) = (x - 5)^2 + 2$
15. $f(x) = (x - 2)^2 - 6$
16. $f(x) = (x + 6)^2 + 3$
17. $f(x) = -(x + 3)^2 - 8$
18. $f(x) = -(x - 4)^2 + 10$
19. $f(x) = 2(x + 3)^2 - 7$
20. $f(x) = 3(x - 2)^2 + 6$
21. $f(x) = 4(x - 1)^2 - 8$
22. $f(x) = 2(x - 1)^2 - 14$
23. $f(x) = -5(x - 2)^2 - 5$
24. $f(x) = 6(x + 4)^2 - 6$
25. 5 ft, $\frac{1}{4}$ sec
26. $h(x) = -\frac{3}{25}(x - 5)^2 + 6$, 6 ft
27. $h(x) = -\frac{1}{20}(x - 20)^2 + 20$, 20 ft, 40 ft
28. 40 ft over, 15 ft up

■ **Lesson 12.5**

7.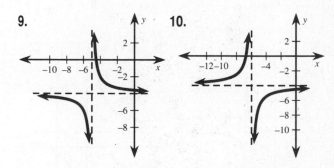

8.

9.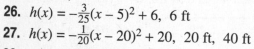

10.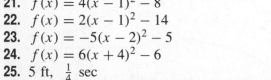

11.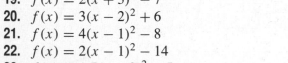

12.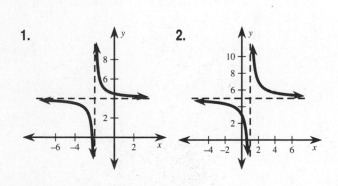

1.

2.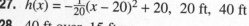

13. $f(x) = -\frac{3}{x+6} + 1$

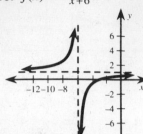

14. $f(x) = -\frac{5}{x-1} + 1$

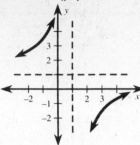

23. $f(x) = -\frac{14}{x+3} + 3$

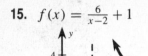

24. $f(x) = -\frac{5}{x+4} + 2$

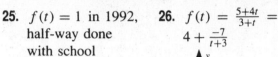

15. $f(x) = \frac{6}{x-2} + 1$

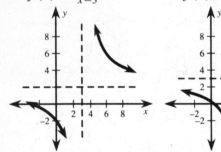

16. $f(x) = \frac{5}{x-3} + 3$

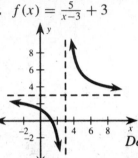

25. $f(t) = 1$ in 1992, half-way done with school

26. $f(t) = \frac{5+4t}{3+t} = 4 + \frac{-7}{t+3}$

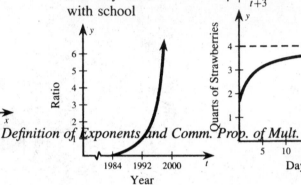

Definition of Exponents and Comm. Prop. of Mult.

17. $f(x) = \frac{12}{x-3} + 2$

18. $f(x) = \frac{11}{x-4} + 3$

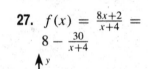

27. $f(x) = \frac{8x+2}{x+4} = 8 - \frac{30}{x+4}$

28. $f(x) = \frac{6x+15}{x} = 6 + \frac{15}{x}$

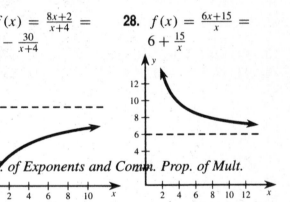

Def. of Exponents and Comm. Prop. of Mult.

19. $f(x) = -\frac{1}{x-4} - 2$

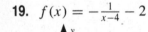

20. $f(x) = -\frac{11}{x+4} + 2$

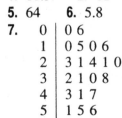

■ **Lesson 12.6**

1. 11.5   **2.** 12   **3.** 235   **4.** 28
5. 64   **6.** 5.8
7.

0	0 6
1	0 5 0 6
2	3 1 4 1 0
3	2 1 0 8
4	3 1 7
5	1 5 6

0, 6, 10, 10, 15, 16, 20, 21, 21, 23, 24, 30, 31, 32, 38, 41, 43, 47, 51, 55, 56

21. $f(x) = -\frac{13}{x+3} + 5$

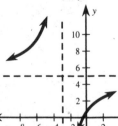

22. $f(x) = \frac{8}{x+2} - 3$

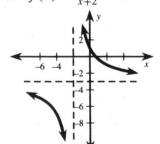

■ **Lesson 12.6 (continued)**

8.

11	1
12	3 5 1 3
13	8 7 8
14	4
15	6 3 6
16	4 8
17	2 1 9
18	3

111, 121, 123, 123, 125, 137, 138, 138, 144, 153, 156, 156, 164, 168, 171, 172, 179, 183

9.   **10.**

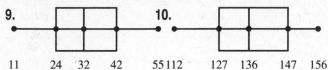

11   24   32   42   55 112   127   136   147   156

11.

59	1
26	7
15	9
14	7
12	2
11	1
10	4
9	7 7 8
8	4 2 7 5
7	0 7 1 0 7
6	8

591, 267, 159, 147, 122, 111, 104, 98, 97, 97, 87, 85, 84, 82, 77, 77, 71, 70, 70, 68

12.

73	7
34	4
29	9
17	1
16	5
11	0
10	0 4
9	4 5
8	5
7	6 8 5 6
6	5 5 0 0
5	8

73.7, 34.4, 29.9, 17.1, 16.5, 11.0, 10.4, 10.0, 9.5, 9.4, 8.5, 7.8, 7.6, 7.6, 7.5, 6.5, 6.5, 6.0, 6.0, 5.8

13. 8.8, 8.6, 8.6, 8.5, 8.1, 7.1, 7.0, 6.6, 6.2, 6.1, 5.9, 5.9, 5.8, 5.7

■ **Lesson 12.7**

1. Mean: 78.45, median: 79.5, mode: 76
2. Mean: $\approx$11,375, median: 8878, mode: none
3. Mean: $\approx$1.3, median: 1, mode: 1
4. Mean: 10.7, median: 8, mode: 4

■ **Lesson 13.1**

1. 5   **2.** 13   **3.** $\approx$2.24
4. $\approx$7.07   **5.** $\approx$10.05   **6.** $\approx$9.06
7. $\approx$12.53   **8.** $\approx$1.41   **9.** $\approx$3.61   **10.** $\approx$2.24
11. $\approx$8.54   **12.** $\approx$3.61   **13.** Yes   **14.** No
15. Yes   **16.** No   **17.** No   **18.** Yes
19. (3, 7)   **20.** (5, $-$2)   **21.** ($-$2, $-$5)
22. (6, $-$4)   **23.** ($-$3, 6)   **24.** ($-$1, $\frac{5}{2}$)
25. ($-$4, $\frac{3}{2}$)   **26.** ($\frac{5}{2}$, $-$1)   **27.** ($-\frac{3}{2}$, $-\frac{1}{2}$)
28. ($\frac{5}{2}$, $\frac{3}{2}$)   **29.** ($-\frac{5}{2}$, $\frac{9}{2}$)   **30.** ($-\frac{3}{2}$, $-\frac{11}{2}$)
31. $\approx$60.83 ft   **32.** $\approx$288 mi   **33.** \$725,000
34. Midpoints of diagonals are the same.
($\frac{11}{2}$, $\frac{3}{2}$)

■ **Lesson 13.2**

1. $4\sqrt{5}$ **2.** $7\sqrt{2}$ **3.** $3\sqrt{6}$ **4.** $\frac{4}{5}$
5. 1   **6.** $\frac{\sqrt{3}}{5}$ **7.** $\frac{2\sqrt{5}}{7}$ **8.** $\sqrt{2}$
9. $\frac{\sqrt{2}}{2}$ **10.** $\frac{4\sqrt{2}}{3}$ **11.** $\frac{5\sqrt{3}}{3}$ **12.** $\frac{2\sqrt{6}}{9}$
13. $3\sqrt{2}$ **14.** $2\sqrt{21}$ **15.** $5\sqrt{2}$ **16.** 63
17. $\frac{5}{9}$ **18.** 40   **19.** $\frac{9}{2}$ **20.** $\frac{5\sqrt{3}}{3}$
21. $4\sqrt{2}$ **22.** $\frac{\sqrt{15}}{5}$ **23.** $\frac{\sqrt{5}}{10}$ **24.** $3\sqrt{2}$
25. $3\sqrt{10} \approx 9.49$ **26.** $12\pi \approx 37.68$
27. $4\sqrt{2}\pi \approx 17.76$ **28.** $5\sqrt{17}$ in. $\approx$20.62 in.
29. $\frac{500}{39}\sqrt{21} \approx 58.75$, $\frac{10}{3}\sqrt{210} \approx 48.30$, $20\sqrt{6} \approx$ 48.99, $\frac{2000}{7} \approx 285.71$

■ **Lesson 13.3**

1. $6\sqrt{3}$ **2.** $9\sqrt{5}$ **3.** $4\sqrt{2}$
4. $-3\sqrt{6}$ **5.** $3\sqrt{5}$ **6.** $-2\sqrt{3}$
7. $7\sqrt{2}$ **8.** $-\sqrt{3}$ **9.** $3\sqrt{2}$
10. $2\sqrt{7}$ **11.** $-2\sqrt{2}$ **12.** $-5\sqrt{10}$
13. $6 + \sqrt{10}$ **14.** $\sqrt{35}$ **15.** $6\sqrt{2} - 8\sqrt{3}$
16. $7 + 4\sqrt{3}$ **17.** $21 - 8\sqrt{5}$
18. $19 - 6\sqrt{2}$ **19.** $17 + 4\sqrt{15}$ **20.** -2
21. 4   **22.** $4 + 3\sqrt{3}$ **23.** $3\sqrt{5} - 5$
24. $9\sqrt{6} - 22$ **25.** Yes   **26.** No   **27.** No
28. Yes   **29.** No   **30.** Yes
31. $\approx$7071;

$\approx$7071, $\approx$7294, $\approx$7510, $\approx$7720, $\approx$7925, $\approx$8124, $\approx$8319, $\approx$8509, $\approx$8695, $\approx$8877
32. $P = 8\sqrt{7} + 16$ **33.** $\approx$61.5 ft

$A = 21 + 24\sqrt{7}$

■ **Lesson 13.4**

1. 25   **2.** No solution   **3.** 5
4. 32   **5.** -27 **6.** No solution
7. 69   **8.** 6   **9.** $\frac{7}{4}$

10. No solution   **11.** $-\frac{39}{10}$ **12.** $-\frac{3}{7}$ **13.** 3
14. 3   **15.** 2   **16.** No solution   **17.** 3
18. 2, 4   **19.** 7, 2   **20.** $\frac{5}{2}$, $\frac{3}{2}$
21. No solution   **22.** $\frac{5}{8}$ **23.** 4   **24.** 4
25. $48\pi \approx 151$ square inches   **26.** $r = 1$ in.
27. 2,415,000   **28.** ≈ 14 ft

■ **Lesson 13.5**

1. $\tan A = \frac{3}{2}$, $\tan B = \frac{2}{3}$
2. $\tan A = \frac{\sqrt{3}}{3}$, $\tan B = \sqrt{3}$
3. $\tan A \approx 0.49$, $\tan B \approx 2.05$
4. $B = 50°$, $b \approx 9.53$, $c \approx 12.45$
5. $B = 67°$, $a \approx 1.70$, $c \approx 4.35$
6. $B = 79°$, $b \approx 25.72$, $c \approx 26.20$
7. ≈ 9.9 ft   **8.** ≈ 45 ft
9. ≈ 741 miles; ≈ 894 miles

■ **Lesson 13.6**

1. $a(b + c + d) = a((b + c) + d)$ *Associative Property*
$\quad\quad = a(b + c) + ad$ *Distributive Property*
$\quad\quad = ab + ac + ad$ *Distributive Property*

2. $(a + b)^2 = (a + b)(a + b)$ *Definition of Exponents*
$\quad\quad = (a + b)a + (a + b)b$ *Distributive Property*
$\quad\quad = a \cdot a + b \cdot a + a \cdot b + b \cdot b$ *Distributive Property*
$\quad\quad = a^2 + ab + ab + b^2$
$\quad\quad = a^2 + 1(ab) + 1(ab) + b^2$ *Multiplicative Identity Axiom*
$\quad\quad = a^2 + (1 + 1)(ab) + b^2$ *Distributive Property*
$\quad\quad = a^2 + 2ab + b^2$ $1 + 1 = 2$

3. $(a - b)^2 = (a - b)(a - b)$ *Definition of Exponents*
$\quad\quad = (a - b)(a + (-b))$ *Subtraction Rule*
$\quad\quad = (a - b)a + (a - b)(-b)$ *Distributive Property*
$\quad\quad = (a + (-b))a + (a + (-b))(-b)$ *Subtraction Rule*
$\quad\quad = a \cdot a + (-b)a + a(-b) + (-b)(-b)$ *Distributive Property*
$\quad\quad = a^2 + (-ab) + (-ab) + b^2$
$\quad\quad = a^2 + (1)(-ab) + (1)(-ab) + b^2$ *Property of Multiplication*
$\quad\quad = a^2 + (1 + 1)(-ab) + b^2$ *Distributive Property*
$\quad\quad = a^2 + 2(-ab) + b^2$ *1 + 1 = 2*
$\quad\quad = a^2 - 2ab + b^2$ *Property of Multiplication*

4. $(-1)(a) + a = (-1)(a) + (1)(a)$ *Multiplicative Identity Axiom*
$\quad\quad = (a)(-1) + (a)(1)$ *Commutative Property of Multiplication*
$\quad\quad = a(-1 + 1)$ *Distributive Property*
$\quad\quad = a(0)$ *Inverse Property of Addition*
$\quad\quad = 0$ *Property of Multiplication*
$\quad\quad = -a + a$ *Inverse Property of Addition*

So, $(-1)(a) = -a$ because $(-1)(a) + a = -a + a$, $(-1)(a) = -a$.

5. $(-a)(-b) = (-1)(a)(-1)(b)$ *Property of Multiplication (Exercise 4)*

            $= (-1)(-1)(a)(b)$ *Commutative Property of Multiplication*

            $= ab$ *Property of Multiplication*

6. $(-a)(b) = (-1)(a)(b)$ *Property of Multiplication (Exercise 4)*

            $= (a)(-1)(b)$ *Commutative Property of Multiplication*

            $= (a)(-b)$ *Property of Multiplication (Exercise 4)*

7. Answers vary.   **8.** Answers vary.

9. $\frac{0}{0}$ is undefined.   **10.** Answers vary.

11. Area I + Area II = Total Area

     $a \cdot b + a \cdot c - a(b + c)$

12. Area I + Area II + Area III = Total Area

     $ab + ac + ad = a(b + c + d)$

13. Subtraction is not commutative in Step 3.

14. In Step 3, $-a + a \neq -(a + a)$